The Abyss

BY THE SAME AUTHOR

Human Behavior in the Concentration Camp

The Abyss

A Confession by

ELIE A. COHEN

Translated by James Brockway

W · W · NORTON & COMPANY · INC ·

NEW YORK

FIRST EDITION

Library of Congress Cataloging in Publication Data
Cohen, Elie Aron.
    The abyss; a confession.
      1. World War, 1939–1945—Prisoners and prisons,
German.   2. World War, 1939–1945—Personal narratives,
Jewish.   3. Cohen, Elie Aron. I. Title.
D805.G3C56513 1973   940.54′72′43 [B]   73–6718
ISBN 0–393–074773

1 2 3 4 5 6 7 8 9 0

Contents

Illustrations

Translator's Introduction

DR. ELIE ARON COHEN was born on July 16, 1909, in the town of Groningen, in the north of the Netherlands, where he studied medicine at the State University.

He became a general practitioner in the village of Aduard, west of Groningen, in 1936, a situation which lasted until May 1, 1941, from which date on he—like all Jewish doctors—was forbidden by the German Occupation authorities to treat non-Jewish patients. He became apprenticed to the trade of orthopedic instrument maker until his arrest on August 13, 1942, when attempting to flee abroad.

After being in an Amsterdam prison and the concentration camp at Amersfoort, he was in the Jews' Assembly Camp at Westerbork from December 8, 1942, to September 14, 1943. On the latter date he was put on a transport to Auschwitz with his family, his wife and son of four being sent straight to the gas chamber on arrival.

He worked as a prisoner-doctor until January 18, 1945, when Auschwitz was evacuated. The "death march" to Mauthausen followed, and from Mauthausen he went to Melk (in Austria). At the beginning of April he was evacuated from Melk to Ebensee, which was liberated by the Americans on May 6, 1945.

Back in the Netherlands, Dr. Cohen worked as an assistant in the Zonnestraal Sanitarium in Hilversum, setting up as a general practitioner again, this time in Arnhem, on May 5, 1947.

On March 11, 1952, he was awarded the degree of doctor at the State University at Utrecht. His professor was Dr. H. C. Rümke and his dissertation was entitled "Human Behavior in the Concentration Camp: A Medical and Psychological Study." This work has been published outside the Netherlands as well, in London, New York, Stockholm, and Tokyo. Dr. Cohen has contributed to several newspapers and journals on the "post–concentration-camp syndrome." He is at present a school doctor in Arnhem. He remarried after the war and has two children.

Dr. Cohen's book grew out of interviews he gave to a popular Dutch weekly and this accounts for its natural, conversational tone. The story he has to tell is both exciting and terrible. Countless books have been published since World War II about life in the Nazi concentration camps, but this one has a special message. Dr. Cohen calls his book "an admonitory monument" —designed to warn us of the depths to which human nature can, in certain circumstances, descend. There is drama in the events he recounts—his going into hiding as a young Jewish doctor in occupied Holland, his abortive attempt to get away to Sweden with his wife and little son, his capture, imprisonment, interrogation, followed by the descent into the abyss of the concentration and extermination camps. But Dr. Cohen survived. He survived even Auschwitz, and the importance of his book lies in his honest analysis of the reasons for his survival.

Dr. Cohen came through because, as a medical man, he had qualifications which could be made use of in the concentration camps, and because, like many others, he was willing to put them to use there. As a realist, he saw clearly that this was his only chance, if chance there still was, of coming out alive. At the same time he was aware of what he was doing. He was aware of the system the Nazis had devised to force their victims to collaborate in the work of their own destruction.

Now, thirty years or so later, Dr. Cohen's book is still topical and of great significance. For it reveals how human beings act in desperate circumstances—the will to survive being stronger than moral scruples; and, more important still, it shows how human beings are capable of operating a system while closing their eyes to its horror. The mechanics of the system take over so that it is no longer a case of men running a system but of a system running men. This did not apply only to the Germans under Nazism—it applied even to their main victims, the Jews.

This is a book which should be read by all who realize that the price of freedom is not only eternal vigilance but also fearless insight into human nature. It is also a deeply human testimony.

James Brockway

Preface

THIS "EGO DOCUMENT" is *my* testimony. In it I am trying, in an emotional way, to understand my own deeds, and in doing so, I have tried hard to be honest. I must ask people to accept that I have had no intention of hurting or insulting anyone or of being unpleasant to anyone. If, unwittingly, I have done so all the same, I am sincerely sorry for it.

Those who would condemn me should realize that only those who have traveled the same road, or almost the same road, are qualified to do so. Those who have not experienced the unimaginable suffering in the German concentration camps, who have never known what it is to be filthy, lice-ridden, hurt, humiliated, and starved, who have not lived in "the kingdom of the dead," lack all right to judge.

Precisely because there is a chance that mankind might forget, precisely because we know that the concentration camp system has not disappeared, this ego document seeks to be an *admonitory monument* which will continue to remind us of the depths of misery, madness, and criminality to which man is capable of descending.

E.A.C.

The Abyss

1

The First Shocks

WHETHER HITLER's coming to power was such a shock
to me personally, I can't even say. I became a Zionist
after reading a small book by Pinsker, entitled *Self-
Emancipation*, and actually we knew all about anti-
Semitism and what you had to do about it. Or rather:
what you *didn't* have to do. For instance, I never rode
around with those "Boycott" stickers on my bike as lots
of people were already doing at the time. As a Zionist,
you said: There's no combating anti-Semitism, for what
you fight against in one place only springs up again
somewhere else. The only thing to be done is to build
up a Jewish country of your own.

An awful lot of things changed in Professor Polak
Daniëls's clinic for internal diseases in Groningen in
those days. Polak Daniëls was a Jewish professor married to an Aryan. He was to be my academic supervisor
when I was studying the electrocardiogram to obtain
the degree of doctor of medicine. I'd begun this work
around 1939 but during 1940 our conversations turned
more and more to the war. And there came a moment—
it was in April 1940, after Hitler's invasion of Norway

and Denmark—when Polak Daniëls said to me, "What
are you going to do when the Germans come here?"

"I don't know yet, professor," I said, "but I think I'll
stay put." (I was a general practitioner in the village
of Aduard, outside Groningen, at the time.)

"You mustn't do that," he said. "You can get through
the Red Cross lines. I can give you a pass so that you
can always get through with your wife and child. Then
you'll be behind the Water Lines." (Those were Holland's defense lines, where dykes could be flooded, and
he was chairman of the Dutch Red Cross.)

I said, "Yes, professor, but then I'll be sitting pretty
behind the Water Lines and a few days later, a fortnight, say, the *Moffen* [our term for the Germans] will
be there too."

He then said, "Do you know what *I* shall do when
things get to be like you're now saying?"

No, I didn't.

"My wife and I will then commit suicide," he said.
"And we shall be taking our dog with us into the grave,
and my children [he had a son and daughter] will have
to decide for themselves—they're grown-up people."

There had already been something strange going on
in Groningen. For instance, there was a Medical Students' Society and suddenly it had convened a big
meeting. This was back in 1933 and it was rumored that
hundreds of German Jews would be coming to study at
the University of Groningen. A stand was taken against
this: foreigners ought not to come and study here just
as they pleased. It would mean the butter on our bread

would be spread thinner still. It's difficult to visualize at the moment, but in those days doctors weren't having so good a time of it as they are now. I resisted this move, but I lost out, of course. It hadn't anything to do with anti-Semitism, they assured me. No, absolutely not. Then Polak Daniëls got to hear of it and he summoned the society's chairman to his room. And he was quite satisfied with the situation when the man said, "No, professor, it is not a move against Jewish students but against all foreign students, no matter from what country."

In the meantime my study was nearing its end. I was engaged to be married. And we seriously considered going to Palestine when I had passed my doctor's exams. We talked about it in full earnest, but, oh well, you know how it is. You've your parents and your parents-in-law—the entire family was living in Groningen. And I allowed myself to be tempted by the fleshpots of Egypt—which exerted more attraction than what Palestine had to offer. I was quite ambitious too. I had become a medical practitioner, and in the family I come from that counted as the highest ideal on earth. My father, you see, was a waiter, in a café frequented by many doctors and intellectuals, and he had encouraged me to study medicine.

It was through that café that I had already taken a different path. I was at the ordinary secondary school and the headmaster of this school and the headmaster of the high school had some lodge meeting or other in that café once a week. Then my father asked the

secondary school man whether I could leave it and go
to the high school—I was in the second grade at the
time. I could change, if I agreed to enter the high school
at the first grade. I then did something that actually
was very cheeky. That's to say, I had heard that a boy
from the first grade at the secondary school had gone
into the first grade at the high school. And me then—
out of the second grade into the first too? I didn't think
that fair. I told the headmaster of the secondary school
this, he conferred with the headmaster of the high
school, and the result was that I was allowed to enter
the second grade at the high school, if I brushed up
my math. This I did, and I managed it, though it was
devilishly difficult.

I passed my high school finals and I was very
bucked about that. It was 1927 and I went looking for a
job. There was a vacancy at a clothes factory. I shouldn't
be earning anything, but I'd get twenty-five guilders—
roughly eight dollars—a month's pocket money, as an
encouragement. Well, I considered that far beneath me;
a high school type didn't do such a thing.

My father had always wanted me to become a doctor. (You didn't "study medicine" in those days—you
"became a doctor.") Yes, become a doctor. But there
had to be money. We weren't all that badly off, but if
you were going to study medicine, you needed a micro-
scope costing two hundred guilders and a dissecting kit
and other things. Then I got a few scholarships from
the Jewish Fund (I was too late, of course, for the big

State Scholarship) and from a study fund belonging to that school I'd been to, the City High School in Groningen. This eased things up considerably, and naturally I acted correctly and paid it all back later on. The reason I didn't at first want to study was genuinely because I didn't want to be a burden to my parents.

And now, why didn't I go to Palestine later on? Yes—that was definitely on account of status in the first place: in the Netherlands you were a doctor. It has always remained a sore spot, dammit, for me—that my father had been nothing but a waiter. When I was a student I couldn't become a member of the exclusive students' club. Oh yes, I would have been allowed to for only 10 per cent of the actual subscription fee. But I didn't fancy that idea either. I was too proud for that. But it was a terribly sore point with me, not to be able to be proud of my father. I often tell my children . . . no, that's not quite honest, for I've never spoken to them outright about it, like this. . . .

When I started studying medicine I was once walking in the market square somewhere and caught sight of my father approaching in the distance, dressed in his waiter's suit, and I crossed over with another chap I was with to the other side of the street. That man, my father, saw it. I had a small attic room in our house in Folkinge Street and one afternoon as I was sitting studying there, my mother came in and said, "You've hurt us a lot. You were ashamed to acknowledge your father."

Naturally, I said I hadn't seen him.

Then she said, "Well, I only hope there's one thing you'll hold on to all your life and that is: whatever you may become, you will never deny your father and mother."

And I have truly kept to that ever since.

In those days a time came when you began to keep your parents as they grew old. I recall how my grandfather used to travel from one of his children to the other, staying two months with each one. My other grandfather lived in the house of one of his children permanently, and every week my father would go and take them about two and a half guilders (about forty cents) to help toward his keep. Nowadays you no longer have any obligation to your parents, since the State takes care of everything. Maybe it was merely an excuse, but this was one of the arguments for my not going to Palestine, to repay my parents, as it were, for allowing me to study.

I had, that's to say, made them a solemn promise. On their twenty-fifth wedding anniversary there was a party. I was already half-qualified as a doctor and I made the opening speech. I said I was extremely grateful for what they had done and that I promised there and then, in public, that when I was earning—I had four guilders a week pocket money at the time—I should look upon it as my duty to make their old age bearable.

So, taken altogether, there were plenty of excuses for not going to Palestine.

I eventually became a general practitioner in Ad-

uard and this went off very well. There was no discrimination against Jews—rather the contrary. Fifty per
cent of my patients were strict Calvinists and the rest
were made up of members of the Orthodox Protestant
Church and Latitudinarians. And to the Calvinists and
Orthodox Protestants you counted as one of God's
Chosen People. So there was no anti-Semitism there.
There was, however, by the time I left. Then the head
of the Christian Primary School called to see me in my
consulting room and said he'd like a word with me. (By
this time I had already received notice that, being a
Jew, I had to relinquish my practice.)

"I've come to save you," he says.

"That's very nice of you," I say. "But how, exactly?"

He says, "Look, in St. Matthew it says: Thy blood
descend on us and our children. [That's what the Jews
are supposed to have said.] And if you will now acknowledge our Saviour, you will then have the as-
surance [he didn't mean the *political* assurance] of
being eternally saved. And I want to help you in this."

I thanked him sincerely for his gesture.

The farmers there in Groningen were not so good
as in Friesland. The Groningen farmer is very jealous
of his capital and his farm, but it was the liberals who
were the least good of all. The others were really very
good. We had table silver hidden away somewhere and
I got every bit of it back, right down to the last tea-
spoon. What's more—the people had kept it polished
every week.

In 1940 I went to Muntendam, the public health
inspector in Groningen—now Professor Muntendam—
and said to him, "If war comes, I want to try to escape
with my wife and son. But I can't abandon my practice
just like that. Would you, as a colleague, see to it that
someone comes—as a *locum tenens*, if I should be out
of the country, or as owner, I don't care how, just as
long as the people aren't left without a doctor."

He promised he would.

The first shock came on November 11, 1939. We
were visiting a psychiatrist, Dr. Weinberg, and someone
came storming in with the news: "They've closed the
frontier. They say the Germans are going to attack tonight." Our visit ended there and then. The Weinbergs
already had a "Capitalist Certificate" for Palestine and
they fled behind the Water Lines. But it turned out to
be a false alarm.

Then came May 9, 1940. Again, all leave cancelled.
My father-in-law, who was a very levelheaded man, said,
"I don't really understand what you are getting so excited
about. [I was evidently pretty nervous.] We had this
sort of thing about twenty to thirty times during World
War I. This is only the fourth time, so we've still plenty
in hand. What are you getting so het-up about? Everything turned out all right then, and it'll go off all right
again this time too."

No, we didn't know with absolute certainty that the
Jews would be persecuted here as well. But we did, of
course, have the examples from Germany. German Jews
came to Groningen. At a given moment in those days

my father or my father-in-law said, "It can't possibly be
that they're just persecuting the Jews like that in Germany. They must be a bad type of person that's involved, anyway." They could not grasp that it was a
clear case of persecution simply for being Jewish. They
were still thinking in terms of punishment and fines.
They had great difficulty in accepting it. Besides, those
German Jews irritated them too. Not me. In any case,
in my circle people thought there must be something
wrong somewhere with those German Jews.

May 9. Before returning to Aduard, I drove past the
army barracks with my wife. I thought that if anything
was going on, I would be able to see it near the barracks. But what did I know? I'd never been in the army.
There was nothing to be seen. The lights were on. At
about eleven thirty or midnight I listened to the radio
again. Nothing was happening.

The next morning, May 10, at quarter to eight—in
the country there, my surgery was at nine—the district
nurse came in and I heard her in the hall, saying to our
servant girl, "What? Are the doctor and his wife still
asleep? Don't they know what's going on?"

"What is it, nurse?" I called. "Come in."

"Don't you know there's a war on?" she said.
"Haven't you heard anything? Did you hear the bridge
being blown up?"

We had heard nothing of all this.

By the time I was dressed it was already nine
o'clock. I rang Groningen. My parents-in-law already
knew. They were to go to Amstelveen, just outside Am-

sterdam, and had risen early, but all public transport
had ceased to run. We made no attempt to get away.
We'd already heard that all the roads had been blocked
and that nobody was being allowed to cross the En-
closure Dyke.

Muntendam kept his word. At ten o'clock he rang
to see if Cohen was still there. Yes, I was still there.

"Well," he said, "do you still want to get away? Because I can send someone."

But I said, "I'm not going. Here I am and here I'm
staying."

Yet that day I didn't really dare hold a surgery.
That gave me a horribly unpleasant feeling. That day
or the next the Germans had already penetrated to
Groningen in force. My father-in-law came, because I
didn't dare drive alone in the car. And so I visited my
patients with him. And I thought, H'm, it's not so bad.
For I had expected to be grabbed at once and maybe
stood up against a wall—well, you know: any damn
crazy thing.

So I stayed there. It will have been in June roughly
that the mayor came along and said, "Doctor, I have
to ask you a very painful question."

And now comes the idiotic thing. I said, "I know
what you want to ask me, Mr. Mayor." What then?
"Whether all four of my grandparents were Jews."

Then he says, "Yes."

I say, "They were."

"In that case," says he, "you are no longer allowed
to be a member of our Air Raid Precautions team."

That was true, officially, though it had no significance whatever. But what made me say right away that all four of my grandparents were Jews and so pin myself down like that? It was misplaced pride.

I have always owned to being a Jew and have never felt "Jew" to be a dirty word. It was that, but I had gradually grown out of that attitude, thanks to my Zionist philosophy. I never spoke about "Israelites," and if people went to speak to me about "Israelites," they always stuttered, because it was such a difficult word in Dutch.

Just one more word about that discrimination. There was indeed discrimination, in a very remarkable way. Precisely because I spoke so naturally about Jews, people sometimes forgot themselves. For example, someone once said to me, "Yes, doctor, the Jews. It's a difficult subject, isn't it? Difficult. But do you know who are much worse? The white Jews!"

That was an idea I was unfamiliar with, and I asked him what he meant.

"Well," he said, "they are our own people, Christians, who also lie and deceive. You don't expect *them* to. They're awful people. They're the white Jews. You expect it from a real Jew."

Crazy, really, eh?

Yes, so I said to the mayor I was a Jew. Life simply went on as before during the first six months. Everyone was saying, "You see, these Germans are better than we thought. They're not too bad, if you treat them properly."

We went on holiday with friends of ours, to Dieren,

and the husband and I then went on to Amsterdam by
bike. We stayed in a hotel in Hilversum where there
were SS men walking about quietly, and we were not at
all afraid. For, well, you know . . . nobody did anything to you.

Then, in November, the mayor called on me again.
And he said, "Doctor, I have to ask you that same question."

"That's all right, Mr. Mayor," I said. "You know the
answer."

"Yes," he said. "And so from today on you must re-
gard yourself as fired from your job as municipal
doctor."

All Jewish civil servants were being dismissed during those days.

Then came that notorious day, February 8, 1941.
The letter from the Germans, saying that as a doctor
you had to be able to declare you were an Aryan. It
was grim, that morning. I can still see myself standing
there in the dispensary—I had one at my home—with
that slip of paper in my hand. I wept . . . because you
were so powerless.

"And now what?" my wife asked.

Yes—I didn't know myself. I had to cease practicing
by May 1. My wife was tougher than I at the time.
Women often are.

2

Our Attempt to Escape

THEY SWOOPED on my practice like vultures on carrion. The Aryans. They all wanted to take it over. And when I asked them on what terms, they would reply, "The usual terms. You know that, anyway. It's been announced by the Medical Association."

I cannot speak for others, but this Medical Association completely let me down. At no time did I ever receive any help from it. We had local branch meetings, at the Faun, a café in Groningen. In November or the beginning of December 1940, those signs saying "Jews Not Admitted" began to appear. I then wrote to the branch secretary, saying that since this sign was also now hanging in the Faun café, I could no longer attend the association's gatherings. I received a very laconic letter in reply, saying that it was true, and that he regretted it as well, but that, yes, in future I should no longer be able to go along. And . . . he wished me all the best. Later on, that Medical Contact body was set up, and *they* seem to have done something, but it came too late for me. But in the days I'm speaking of you were . . . well . . . let down, dropped. And you were allowed to hand over your practice only on the usual terms. [Dr. Cohen eventually hired his practice out to a respectable doctor, who finally took it over from him in 1945.]

Those weeks up to May 1, 1941, were very difficult weeks but also very nice weeks. It always seems to be the same—that you're not really appreciated until you begin to take leave of people. Lots of people behaved extremely kindly during those days. They were sorry I was going. There was no celebration, of course.

My wife rented a house in Groningen and we moved there on May 1. I nailed a board to the door reading "Doctor." I think I was the third or fourth Jewish doctor there—rather a lot for a few thousand Jews. I went to the University Hospital—a thing that was also forbidden actually—and started work as an apprentice with a firm called Van Halsema, which manufactured arch supports for the feet and other appliances. I learned how to make these supports, and some smelting and so on, just to have something to do. As far as we were concerned, 1941 was the same for us as for everyone: nothing much to mention. There was one big alarm in Groningen, in October 1941, when the Germans suddenly organized raids on Jews. They were already active in the Achterhoek, farther south, and in the town of Zwolle just north of there, and we were warned by phone that they were on their way to us. I went into hiding in the house of my predecessor, but it all fizzled out. I was very naïve though. I slept at my parents-in-law's place, in a veranda. I kept a bicycle in it, so that I could ride off as soon as they turned up!

Well, 1942 came. On July 15, 1942, the Jews had to go to the labor camps. I didn't receive a draft notice myself, probably because I had moved house from Aduard to Groningen. And they probably had the lists of May 1940, showing who were Jews. I then "went underground," that is, into hiding, in my own house, never venturing out in the street again. My wife did the shopping and when they asked her, "Where's your husband gotten to?" she would say, "I don't know. He's gone away and I haven't heard a word from him since."

One day my father-in-law comes along to our house with a *mijnheer* who says he is from Amsterdam. This *mijnheer* says, "Your father-in-law's name is in the baptismal records at . . ." (I no longer recall the name of the place—it was somewhere in Friesland.)

"That's fine for my father-in-law," I said, "but it doesn't help us any. It may mean my wife is only half-Jewish, but she married a full Jew, so according to the regulations, she still counts as Jewish."

He then said, "Maybe. But there's another way we can help you. We have forged identity cards—they cost a hundred guilders a time. I can get you those, if you like."

It was the end of July, the beginning of August. And I said, "No."

"Why not?" he asked.

I said, "This war'll go on for a long time, and I don't see myself holding out all that time."

"But we can also arrange for you to go underground," he said.

No, I didn't want to go underground.

Now, I must digress for a moment about this business of going underground. We were befriended by a non-Jewish couple in Groningen, both of them biologists, the husband a teacher. I had asked them if they knew of an address where my little boy could go underground, if things came to that pass. The man knew of an address at a colleague's of mine and they were willing to have my son. In July we felt that things had now got to this stage, and so we arranged for our little boy to be taken away. The biologist called on us that same evening and we asked him how it had gone off.

"Oh, fine," he said. "He didn't mind one bit. Only he hasn't gone to Wim's." (Wim was my colleague.)

"Why not?" I asked.

Well, Wim, it turned out, had been a little scared, after all, and so he had found a home for our boy with some Jewish farmers in the area.

"But that comes to the same thing," I said. "Whether he's with that farmer or here with us won't make a scrap of difference. You'll have to return there tomorrow and fetch him back."

This he did. And so our little boy came back to us.

Then, after that, this business with the *mijnheer* about the identity cards came up. I didn't want any of that going underground. It seemed terrible to me to have to spend a few years like that. And besides, I should still be in the Netherlands, in the danger zone.

So I said to the man, "What I'd really like . . . but of course you couldn't fix that . . . is to get abroad."

"I'll talk about it," he said, "and come back and see you again in a couple of days' time."

When he did come back, two days later, he said, "I can fix something up for you. There are some timber boats that sail between Sweden and Delfzijl [that's a little port in the north of the Netherlands] and we'll build a small hold for you in the middle of all that wood, with room enough for three. A German goes on board too, but you'll be outside the three-mile limit within a few hours. The German then leaves the ship and then you'll be free."

I believed him. And that, of course, was terribly stupid of me, ever to have believed a thing like that. I can see that now. For taking timber from Holland to Sweden, that's the same as carrying coals to Newcastle. But I was blinded, of course. I wanted to get away and seized any chance that came my way.

He went on, "But I mustn't organize it myself. The captain'll have to come and see you about it. And we must bribe that German, and that costs money."

"How much?"

"Six thousand guilders a head."

"I haven't got that much," I said.

"Okay," he said. "How much had you in mind?"

"I can lay my hands on thirteen thousand," I said. (I could sell some shares.)

"Okay. But in that case, if you've any jewelry, I'd advise you to take it along with you as well. If you've got any hidden away, I'll go and collect it for you. Then you can sell it in Sweden and live off the proceeds."

No, I didn't ask him if he could identify himself. I trusted him. It was the first time I'd ever had anything to do with a matter like that, and I really trusted him. I even gave him the address where a few things had been stowed away, and he went and collected them . . . a few pearls and some little diamond things.

The next day the captain turned up. He introduced himself as Van Waveren. He told us that at three o'clock on August 13, a taxi would draw up outside with a man in it we could trust. I should then have to remove my yellow star (showing I was a Jew) and this man would drive us to the boat. We should set sail that same evening.

"But," he said, "you must pay some money in advance, of course, because naturally I must keep on good terms with that German soldier who'll be seeing you go on board. And I'd like four thousand guilders to take along with me now."

I gave it him. And then I said something crazy. I said, "*Mijnheer,* how do I really know I can trust you? Who's to say you're not an SS spy?"

Then he said, "Do I look like one?"

Well, what could I say?

"If you want to," he said, "you can go and inquire in Delzijl, that's where the *Göteborg* is moored." The *Göteborg* was the name of the boat.

I didn't go, because I thought it a good argument.

That evening I said to my wife, "Look, actually, we can't be sure of a damn thing. I don't think there's any point in our still trying to go underground anywhere. If they are in league with the Germans, they'll probably be keeping a watch on our house from now on, and it'll be a one-way ticket to the extermination camp at Mauthausen. Then our number will be up."

It was a fairly dramatic conversation we had, the two of us.

We had told my father-in-law and my mother. The Thursday morning before we left my mother called on us.

"Elie," she said, "you've always been a lucky one, you have, and now you're doing this thing, and you're quite right to. I'm sure it'll succeed. But there's one thing more I think you ought to do. Your father ought to know. Otherwise I don't think it's right."

"I agree with you," I said.

We were no longer permitted to board a streetcar or go by bicycle. So my mother then walked back and an hour or so later my father turned up. He was a bit mad at me. I'm laying so much emphasis on this, because it was the last time I saw him. My mother, too, for that matter. But we did at least part as . . . well, as understanding people. The words my mother said . . . I can still hear them, not often, but now and then: "You succeed in everything and you'll succeed in this as well."

We had a meal, it wasn't much that Thursday lunchtime, and then I went and played a bit with my small son, then three years old. We played at marbles. And at three o'clock the taxi came. There was a ring at the door and a man was standing there and saying, "I've come to fetch you."

He smelled of liquor. I didn't like that. But there you are . . . we were in that boat for better or for worse. We got into the taxi. The chauffeur was a former patient of mine. It was a taxi from the Imex Garage in Groningen, and I heard later on that they were hand in hand with the Nazis. So that fits too.

The only people in the know were our neighbors, to whom we'd taken a few more things. They waved us good-by as though they were saying "Bon voyage!"

We had to go to Delfzijl, and this meant driving past the station. Now, in front of the station in Groningen there's a fairly big flower bed, and you can drive straight through from there to Delfzijl. But this man turned to the right, toward the station.

"Why are you taking this way?" I said to him. "You don't have to, do you?"

Then he said, "Yes, I do. I've a suitcase in the left luggage office."

Well, I ask you . . . what does one do?

So the taxi pulled up outside the station, the man got out, and a second later a man came up holding a revolver in his hand and said, "You're under arrest."

We were taken to the "Gestapo House" in Groningen, the Scholtenhuis . . . it was bombed to rubble at the end of the war. The car stopped there, in front of the Scholtenhuis in the market square, and my wife flung open the door and made a run for it. And that

Security Police chap—for that's what he was—went chasing after her. Then I said to the chap at the wheel (it was a Citroën car and I'd had one myself): "Drive on! I've a tidy sum of money on me and you won't regret it."

He said, "Nothing doing."

"All right," I said. "I can understand that. But get from behind that steering wheel then and hand it over to me. I'll leave the car standing somewhere and you'll get it back."

But he wouldn't do that either. So I sat there in that taxi with our little boy.

In the meantime, the man from the Security Police had caught my wife, and so they came back. And then, for the first time, I knew what it was to suffer from shock. I stepped out of the car and my legs gave way beneath me. Inside the Scholtenhuis we had to climb some stairs and I had to do that on my hands and knees. I was completely useless. And I thought, So this is it— this is the end of you.

I had had only a vague presentiment that maybe something might not be in order. They may have known more about it in Amsterdam, but we in Groningen didn't know a thing about these decoys. All the men had gone and there wasn't much left to catch in a trap anyway. I was the first to try to escape that way in Groningen. After I had published my dissertation (after the war, that is) Van der Zwan, a nerve surgeon who now lives in Zwolle, wrote an article in which you can read: "In August 1942, there was a dreadful rumor circulating in Groningen that our colleague Cohen and his family had been arrested when attempting to flee to Sweden."

We were both searched. My wife even had to let down her hair. One of those SS men came into the room, Lehnhof was his name, and he said, "We've caught you at last." I didn't understand a thing. But they were looking for diamonds. My brother-in-law and his father had had a diamond-cutting business in Amsterdam, called Spier and Van Wezel. They'd escaped to England. Spier Senior had always said, "If I leave, I shall have my capital in my waistcoat pocket." And the SD—the Security Police—thought we had Spier's diamonds in *our* keeping, for later on we were taken to Amsterdam, to the Currency Control Command. The man who had arrested us was a certain Schröder. I have often thought since that I ought to try to trace this fellow Schröder, to find out what was behind it all. But I haven't found the courage or the energy to do so.

I was placed under lock and key in the police station in Groningen, in the Martini Cemetery. My wife was in the women's department, myself in the men's. They phoned the Jewish Council (which attended to Jewish affairs during the Occupation) and then that friend we'd been on vacation with came and collected my small son. His name was also Cohen—Jo Cohen— and I'd said to him, "Jo, we're going to flee. Do you want the address too?" Then Jo had said, "No, I'm a member of the Jewish Council, and I don't believe anything's going to happen to me. So I'd rather not."

This man, who had exceptionally keen brains, didn't grasp what was really going on either. It was on June 22, 1943, I think, that I went with him to the Zionist train in the concentration camp at Westerbork. It was when they cancelled the protection enjoyed by the Zionists. I was hauling along his luggage for him and I was weeping, but he wasn't.

"Elie," he said, "What are you getting so upset about? You always look on the black side. Why should you be weeping? They'll put us to work there, and if they do that, they'll be forced to give us food. I really don't understand why you are getting so worked up about it."

(This is yet another proof—and I still insist on this —that we didn't know a thing. We did not know what lay beyond Westerbork. But we did have a vague feeling that it wouldn't be very pleasant.)

Well, this man, Jo Cohen, collected my small boy and took him to my parents.

There was a small table fixed to the wall in my cell supported by a bracket, and I wanted to give up the fight. So I took off my shirt and made a sort of noose of it, which I tied to the bracket. The next day I heard from my wife that she already knew about this and had asked the police if they would keep an extra close watch on me. And when I was making the attempt the light went on in the cell and in came a policeman, who said, "You shouldn't do that, young man. You can never tell how things may work out. You still have your wife and you've a child, after all." That night the light remained burning till morning.

The next day we were transported to Amsterdam.
The policeman who accompanied us said, "You can
choose. You'll be taken by us to Amsterdam. If you will
give your word of honor that you won't try to escape,
we'll dispense with the handcuffs. But if you say you
can't be sure or refuse to give us your word, I'll have to
handcuff you."

I said, "Okay. I won't escape."

Very stupid. We went to the station by streetcar.
The people in the streetcar were very astonished. Jews
allowed in a streetcar! We entered the train. There's a
urinal somewhere outside the station in Amsterdam.
When we got out I told the cop I had to go.

"Okay," he said. "I'll wait here for you. There's no-
where you can get away to in any case."

And there, in that urinal, stood the man who had
come to collect us and who had reeked of liquor. The
Third Man. We did not exchange one word.

We were taken to the Currency Control Command.
At one stage my wife and I were walking twenty yards
behind those policemen. I could have jumped onto a
moving streetcar. I could have done something else. I
had some relatives in Amsterdam, but before I got that
far . . . Besides, they were Jews and that'd mean getting other people into hot water. No, I didn't seriously
think of escaping and neither did my wife. My wife had
to go in for an interrogation and they left me in a room
on my own. I walked to and fro a bit. I wasn't wearing my Jew's star. And at a certain moment an SS man

came in. And he said to me, "What are you doing here?" I was waiting to be heard. "What then? Are you a Jew?" Yes. "Then where's your star?" So, well, I told him about our attempted escape. That man then acquainted me with the first principles of SS behavior. Knocked me about. Not too roughly though. And I had to walk ten times around a balustrade that was there. Afterward my wife said to me, "I heard it and wondered what was going on out there."

All right. I had to go in to that man Schröder's room. And then I suddenly realized how easy it was to tell too much. This Schröder chap didn't even seem such a very bad type to me, in that now and then he shut me up. At one moment I was saying, "And then a friend of ours . . ." And he said, "I don't want to know at all. You don't have to tell me either." Nor did he want to know about the things I had had hidden away. All that concerned him was those diamonds. That was certainly very decent of the chap, because I had gone gabbling away, without any bawling me out and without torture. Really, I was completely knocked out.

After that, I was confined to jail for ten weeks in an Amsterdam prison. During that period we were interrogated again. We were collected by Schröder, my wife and I.

Schröder said, "It's not very nice for you. You haven't seen each other all this time. We're going to the Currency Control Command again. There's a table there and a couple of chairs. If you promise not to escape, I'll let you stay together for a few hours to talk to each other. Because all I have to do is read those interrogation reports out and then you'll have to sign them, and that can take us half an hour or I can make it last four hours. What do you say?"

We said, "All right, let us sit upstairs."

We sat there—I had a beard, as Jews you weren't allowed to be shaven—and another Jew was walking about there—not a prisoner. I asked if he had any cigarettes with him—I hadn't had a smoke in all those weeks.

"Keep quiet, sir, keep quiet," he replied. "I don't know you and I don't want to know you either."

That man was very scared indeed. Well, yes, you had been cut off from the outside world for a bit. You didn't know exactly what had been going on. We had, however, noticed how some nights a lot of streetcars had been moving through the streets. Then someone came in again and he said the Jews had been picked up.

In that cell I had slowly begun to find out what the pattern was. A man was once brought in who owned what were known as the "blue shops" in Amsterdam, a textile dealer. He was completely mixed-up, as everyone was when they first arrived in such a cell.

"I don't understand a thing about it," he said. "A woman came in and asked me if I wanted to escape to England. And I said, maybe I did. And that was sufficient to have me arrested. I'm a stomach patient. And you're a doctor, aren't you? In that case, you must prescribe me a diet."

"Then you must begin," I said, "by eating nothing at all here today."

He didn't mind at all, and *we* were hungry. The food wasn't too bad, but there wasn't enough of it. We kept it up for two or three days until he got wise to it, and said, "You can all drop dead. I'm eating anything I can get my hands on and devil take the consequences."

3

Transport to Amersfoort

IN THE END we were put on a transport. At about five
o'clock in the evening. We asked the guards where we
were bound for.

"You're lucky," they said. "You're staying in the
Netherlands. You're going to Amersfoort."

Now, I had already heard about the camp at Amersfoort from a policeman in Aduard who'd been there
once.

"Doctor," he'd said, "wherever else you may have to
go, try not to land up in Amersfoort. That place is a hell
on earth. If you land up there, you can say good-by. The
things I saw in the short time I was there . . . You
really mustn't go there, believe me. . . ."

And that was where we were going.

But the move was suddenly cancelled. We were
taken to other cells. And in my cell there was Philip
Mechanicus, a Jewish journalist. And he said, "I've got
three cigarettes left." We smoked them between us.
Philip Mechanicus was a brave chap. We were put on
a transport the next day. There were some streetcars
standing in front of the prison and Mechanicus tried to

break through the cordon and make his getaway behind them. But he wasn't quick enough and there were too many people about as well. How they knew a transport was leaving I don't know, but there were lots of them about. They collared him and knocked him about very badly indeed. And in the train to Amersfoort an SS man kept coming up to him and saying, "You'll go through something, you will!" This turned out to be an idle threat, because no special attention was paid to him anymore in Amersfoort.

At about four in the afternoon we walked from the station to the *Polizeiliches Durchgangslager*—the Police Transit Camp—at Amersfoort. And all of a sudden there were such strange thoughts running through my head. You looked into all those rooms—it wasn't blackout time yet and the lights were burning. You could see mothers sitting round the table with their children. In another house they were drinking tea. And all the time I was thinking of what that policeman had said in Aduard. And then I thought, Doesn't the world care then what is going on here? That we are walking, as though it were all perfectly natural, to this camp, maybe to our death? What a strange thing it is that everyone should live so much for himself alone, and that you no longer care what's happening to someone else.

We arrived at the camp. A man was standing beside the gate. And our reception showed us what we might be in for. We saw the labor gangs coming back in at the double. To us they looked practically like corpses. And

an SS man went up to a fellow standing by the gate
and knocked him down and kicked him till he lay there,
unmoving. Probably dead. It was then that I began to
look to my own protection. I called that "depersonaliza-
tion." You looked on, as though through a peephole,
taking no part in things yourself. You watched. It didn't
concern you.

It was too late in the evening to get us into the
clothes—there were military uniforms—and I landed
up in a barrack hut—Number 3 hut. And we walked
about a bit.

There was a young man walking there whom I did
not know and I asked him, "Were you on this transport
too?" (He wasn't a Jew, you see, and our transport had
consisted entirely of Jews.)

"No," he said, "I've been here a good few months
now."

"Why are you in civilian clothes then?" I asked him.

And then he gave me a reply which bore witness to
a state of grace I myself lack completely and shall never
be able to attain.

He said, "I'm in civilian clothes, because I'm to be
executed this evening."

That really shook me. It was the first time I'd heard
this. He asked me if it had shaken me. I admitted it
had. "I think it's terrible," I said. "And you say it so
calmly and so quietly."

"Well," he said, "it's not so bad as you see it. I believe
in Jesus Christ and I am going to my Saviour. And if
that is to happen now, or in thirty years' time, makes no

difference to me. I'm here on account of good works I have done, and I really don't think it's so very terrible."

That, you see, is really an incredible support, being able to look death in the eyes like that. In various books I have read, it says that the pious among the Jews in Poland also went into the gas chamber praying, because they believed in God and believed in justice and in God knows what else. That has never been my portion.

So I was in Amersfoort, and there were advantages, after all, in being on Dutch soil. Advantages the German Jews enjoyed later on, in the German camps, and which we then had no longer. I came across a former patient of mine. We Jews weren't allowed to have any money and so we could never buy anything in the canteen. The non-Jews could. He said to me, "I've ten guilders. I'll give you five, then you can buy something. But you must give it back to me after the war." He never returned. He had been an important figure in the resistance.

I had to join the Jews Squad, and damned hard work it was too. We had to do bricklaying and haul bricks about. I wasn't too skilled at that. You had, for instance, to keep your wheelbarrow straight on what they called a beam. Once my wheelbarrow slipped off the beam. An SS man then came up to me and said, "You're doing that wrong." Yes, I'd grasped that. He showed me how to do it and walked off again. People who'd seen this incident asked me if I had some special influence in the camp or some protector. No. Why?

"That was Father Christmas," they said, "yet he didn't beat you to death. That's what he does to all the others who can't do it right." Well, so I'd been lucky.

Okay then—in the end it went fairly well and we even evolved a special technique for piling up the bricks to make the barrow seem full when it wasn't. Popeye the Sailorman, another SS guard, got wind of this and pounced on it.

I owe my life—absolutely, with no doubt whatever —to the fact that I'd studied medicine. Once, in '42, all of us Jewish doctors in Groningen had refused to examine people for the labor camps. Later on, it appeared that an NSB-er (a member of the Dutch Nazi Party) was doing it. He did it much better and quicker than we did. But we didn't want to do it.

One day in Amersfoort I was busy unloading books from a Calvinist Youth Club. Now, inside the camp there was another camp, of people with American or dual nationality, and I was having to unload these books close to this other camp. Next to the barbed wire a woman was standing and she said, "Couldn't you give me one of those books? We've nothing to read here."

I turned round and said, "No, nurse. [I could see she was wearing a nursing badge.] I daren't. That SS guard's standing too close to us."

"How did you know I was a nurse?" she then asked.

"I'm in the same profession," I said. "I'm a doctor and I recognized your badge."

"Then you must be Dr. Cohen from Aduard," she said. "You were one of Professor So-an-So's assistants in ward number so-and-so. I was there too, as a nurse."

That evening I was called from the parade ground
by Van Zeestraten, the camp superior. He said, "There's
a nurse I assist as medical orderly in the American
camp. She's asked me if I'll protect you. Go and sit
down first and have something to eat."

He gave me some bread and sausage.

"Now, listen to me carefully," he said. "I don't know
a blind thing about all this medical business—you
realize that, don't you? I'm in charge of the ambulance
here and every evening people with all sorts of injuries
come pouring in. I haven't the foggiest idea how to
handle them, but you're a doctor. Will you do that in
the evenings?"

Naturally I said I would.

"Okay," he said, "but in that case you'll have to take
off your jacket, because the *Moffen* mustn't be allowed
to see you're a Jew."

So for several weeks I worked on that ambulance.

I saw De Miranda, the socialist alderman in Amsterdam, beaten to death. He was in that transport from
Amsterdam to Amersfoort with me and they had it in
for that man from the very start. The Communists did
too. They would say to him, "You, who fobbed off
the unemployed with a mere pittance and let them
starve . . ." They went for that man in an incredible
way. But it didn't trouble him in the first few days. In
those days all we had to do was march. In clogs, it's
true, which isn't exactly easy. He was beaten to pulp,
flung on a wheelbarrow, and I had the job of wheeling

him to the parade ground. When I got there I asked the
foreman, "Where must I take this man?" "Oh, just put
him down there," he said, and then they simply threw
him into the mud. He was dead by the evening.

So the first advantage of my being a doctor was that
I worked there during the evening and so got some
food. After a week or two Van Zeestraten said, "That
Jews Squad isn't so good for you. I'm setting up a Corpse
Squad and you'll be the man in charge. You'll have to
collect the corpses here in the camp and bury them."
Well, that's what I did, with a few others. We would
then take the corpses to the small mortuary. There were
three coffins there and we would lay two corpses in
each one, and when they were full we had to take them
to the pit. Arrived there, we tipped up the wheelbar-
rows and then the bodies were buried. Those were the
people who had died or had been beaten to death. You
ask me how that affected me? Not at all. Well, not
much: I *really* was thinking only of myself. I had a
rotten job, and if it was I who carted them off or someone else made no difference. I was mighty pleased to
be out of that Jews Squad, for that surely was a very
notorious one.

But now something crazy. After the war, they asked
me if I would come to Amersfoort to show them where
those corpses had been buried—De Miranda's among
others. I went there—it was in '47—it's completely
crazy, but I could no longer find my way. The trees had
grown taller, the barbed wire had disappeared, there

were different, painted, better-looking barrack huts. It had become a military camp, I believe, and I wasn't able to show them a single thing. They were very disappointed. So was I, but I honestly didn't know anymore.

I had the same thing in Westerbork. I went back there, too, once, with my wife. Now, I'd stayed in that camp for nine months, so you'd think you'd know, in that case. But they had broken up the railroad lines, and the barbed wire had disappeared there as well. Everything was neatly planted. The atmosphere had changed. I no longer knew where the cookhouse had been. I no longer knew where I had worked. Where the clinic had been. I didn't know anything anymore.

Then Van Zeestraten once put me down as suffering from dysentery and so got me a week or more in the sickbay. Among the patients there was a Mr. Mol, from The Hague. I mention that name, because no one has ever been able to tell me anything more about him. One evening, after the doors had been shut, there was a big "military gathering" in the corridor around nine o'clock—there was some lieutenant or other present too —and these people explained to us how the war would be going in future. And Mol then said to me (it was November '42), "Cohen," he said, "there's one thing you must promise me. If we should lose touch with each other in the coming weeks, you're coming to celebrate New Year's Eve at my place in The Hague. Agreed?" Yes, of course it was agreed. That was the only thing you could do to keep your spirits up.

On December 8 a transport was announced which

included me. A number was called too, let's say it was
Number 50. No one responded to it. Everyone excited.
Where had Number 50 gotten to? Where could he be?
Until it was discovered Number 50 was dead. But
they'd reported to the central office, or whatever it was
called, that Number 51 was dead. Number 51 was still
alive, however, and Number 50 was dead. Now, it
seems a simple enough matter to put a thing like that
right. You simply say, "We've made a mistake. We'll
send Number 51 instead." But no—*they* had another
way of doing things. That chap who is officially dead,
but still alive, you kill him off. That's also a way of
solving problems.

Okay then, we had to be on the transport to the
camp at Westerbork. Before we left, a German prisoner
came to us (we thought he was some SS man who had
done something wrong) and asked us if we knew where
we were going to. No, we didn't. He said, "You're going
to Oberhausen, Recklinghausen, Mauthausen."

A man was standing next to me, Bernard Koster, a
diamond merchant. And he said, "Elie, if that chap's
right, it's the mortuary for us."

We were collected by the Dutch Military Police.
And the way they bawled at us! And cursed us! Swore
at us! It was so bad we said to ourselves whether we
were bitten by the cat or the dog, it was all the same.
But once we were on the train at Amersfoort and it had
started, those boys turned round, flung open their knap-
sacks, and said, "We know you're dying of hunger. So
we've brought along some bread for you—get into it!"

Extremely sporting and extremely kind. That train stopped at a few places and they then pulled down the windows and shouted, "Hi there! There are prisoners here from Amersfoort who need something to eat!" And the passengers threw apples in to us, and loaves, just as if it was a kind of vacation trip.

4

We Keep Our Little Boy
with Us

WE ARRIVED IN Hooghalen and had to walk to Wester-bork—at that time the railroad didn't extend that far. And when we got out, I heard someone call, "Is there a Dr. Cohen with you?"

It was a high-ranking German inmate of the camp, Zielke was his name then; he is now living in New York as Wilkie. When I reported to him he said, "Your wife is waiting for you in Westerbork." My wife, that's to say, had been taken straight to Westerbork from the prison in Amsterdam, and myself to Amersfoort. She had already been sitting in the train, waiting to be deported from Westerbork, when she saw a young girl in the train ask some man or other something. So she thought, If she can ask something, so can I. So she said, "Sir, my husband is a doctor and he's in some other place. May I wait for him here?"

And the man went to Gemmeker, the camp com-mandant, and asked him—he was a crazy so-and-so, really. And Gemmeker had said, "All right, let the

woman wait." (Forgetting that I could already have
been beaten to death twenty times over in Amersfoort.)
So, when I arrived, we met. A medical detail is that
during all those months her periods had ceased completely, yet when she saw me, she menstruated at once.
But I was utterly impotent in the first weeks.

I was incarcerated in the penal barrack. There was
one more transport due to leave Westerbork that month
—a thing I, of course, was unaware of at the time. We
had arrived on Tuesday evening and a transport left
on Fridays. I saw Mr. Spier of the Jewish Council and
asked him if he could do anything so that I could stay
on there. And *Mijnheer* Spier was going to do his best.
That Thursday evening, Zielke (Wilkie) came into the
barrack hut (he spoke reasonably good Dutch) and he
said to me, "They've agreed to your staying on here
and that you don't have to go on tonight's transport
train."

Later on I heard what had happened. That man
Zielke had gone to the commandant, Gemmeker, and
said to him, "There's a doctor arrived on this last transport and we need doctors. But he's a punishment case.
May he stay on here?"

Then Gemmeker had said, "As far as I'm concerned
he can stay on all right, but I'll have to get permission
from Groningen, because that's where he was arrested."
And Groningen had said, "Let him stay."

If I had not been a doctor, I should have gone then,
and really not in good condition as regards nutrition,
for all of us were practically skeletons. The only reason

they hadn't been shocked at the sight of us in Westerbork was because a week before a transport had arrived from Ellekom, the training ground of the Dutch
SS, and those people were in a shocking state.

So I was allowed to stay, and the peace of mind it
gave me was such that I didn't hear a thing of the entire
transport which left that night. I didn't hear any names
called out. The next morning, when I woke up, God
only knows what time it was, the entire hut was empty
but for two or three people. The rest had gone. The
shit lay everywhere.

So my little boy, as I have said, had been taken by
the Jewish Council to my parents. And into my parents'
house had come a niece, with a child. Her husband had
been carried off to a labor camp. But during that
notorious night of October 2 to 3, when all the men in
those labor camps were taken to Westerbork, they
picked up all their wives too. They turned up at my
parents' house also, and then they had to go along as
well, with my little boy.

As my father had stayed on at that café-bar for a
time (as long as he was *allowed* to work, that is), he
had come across this German in it. And now he saw this
same man walking to and fro there. He went up to him
and said, "I'm here with my son's little boy, and I've
no idea where my son is. We just can't go on the transport like this." And that German spoke to another German, and they got permission to go back. Later on, of
course, you realize that it's all a game of cat-and-mouse.

My son was taken to my parents-in-law. My parents evidently smelled a rat. I don't know exactly what happened. Then, a few weeks later, my parents were collected from Groningen and transported to Auschwitz in the same week as I was taken to Westerbork. My boy was taken to the home of acquaintances of ours, a "mixed" Jewish couple (one Jewish, the other not). They're people we're still on good terms with.

Then, on April 9, 1943, came the order that all Jews in the provinces had to report. At Vught, I think it was —where there was another camp. In the meantime, I had had so big a promotion in Westerbork that my name was on the *Stammliste*, a list of the privileged, the "regulars." With the red stamp. Well, that was so safe, nothing could *ever* happen! That's what the *Stammliste* was. It formed the very foundations of Westerbork. So I thought, Why should we let my little son go to Vught or go underground? We're as safe as houses here. So we had him join us. At the time, he was suffering from inflammation of the ear—otitis—and had to have an operation in Groningen, in Professor Huizinga's clinic. And now and then my wife or I (they always had to keep one of us as a hostage) was allowed to visit him. The visit was never allowed to last longer than three-quarters of an hour, with a nurse in attendance. The military police who took us to Groningen were very good sports. They said "Okay, go ahead, but you must be back by four"—and they'd mention some place. Well, that's what we did. That half-Jewish couple said to us, "For God's sake, let us

take the little boy. We'll look after him well." But no, I
didn't want to, because we were so secure in Westerbork.

When I was back in Groningen after the war, a
friend said to me, "Eelko Huizinga is very keen to speak
to you." So I went to Eelko Huizinga—he was the
professor in whose clinic the boy had been operated on,
and where I had been allowed to sit with him for just
three-quarters of an hour, in the presence of a nurse.
And Huizinga said, "Cohen, I did something terrible
to you. Will you give me a chance to make up for it?"

"Very well," I said, "but first of all I'd like to know
why you acted so strangely."

"I was afraid," he said. "You can spit at that now, if
you like, and you'd be justified, and you can go for me,
and you'd still be right. I'm terribly sorry about it. Of
course, I can't bring that child back to life for you, but
just ask me what you want. Would you like to become
my assistant?"

"Never," I said, "because I don't want to stay in
Groningen."

"What *do* you want then? Would you like to go to
Amsterdam, or to Leyden? I can take care of it for you."

"All right then," I said. "I'd like to go to Amsterdam"
—never thinking there would really be anything in it.

"Right you are then," he said. "Just wait."

He went away for a while and came back with a
letter. "Now, you go with this letter to Professor De
Kleyn in Amsterdam, and if you want to become an ear,
nose, and throat specialist there, you'll be able to."

That man had simply been afraid that my boy would be kidnaped during our visits to the hospital and that he would be held responsible for it. I mean, I can't even get worked up about it now, because . . . well, people *were* afraid. And he wasn't at all a bad fellow fundamentally, but he didn't dare, and he didn't *see* and . . . well, I was able to get an appointment with Professor De Kleyn. I was already going with my present wife then, and he rang her up a few times to ask whether I was coming to work with him or not, and then I'll have said something like: "He can drop dead. I'm not interested." All of it left me stone cold at the time. It was 1945.

I became a doctor in Westerbork. Every doctor could have his own practice, for the people there were allowed to choose their doctor. Since I climbed the social ladder fairly quickly in Westerbork, I acquired a number of terribly important and powerful functions. In the first place, I became the "transport doctor." That meant that every Monday night I was on duty in the clinic. This was the night before the transport train left for Auschwitz or Sobibor. It usually left Westerbork on a Tuesday. The people were called out in the dead of night. Their superior in the barrack block then called out the names of those who had to leave on the transport. It was then that all the trouble that those people had gone to up till that night (to avoid transportation) proved to have been in vain. Only one possibility then remained —and this, too, was later taken away from us. It was

that a doctor—which meant me—would in the middle
of the night—or rather, at five or six in the morning—
declare them to be "unfit for transport" on the grounds
of illness. And so from five A.M. onward the requests
came pouring in to me to go and see, and then I went,
of course, and as soon as possible. I was then able, for
example, to declare that women who were five months
pregnant were seven months pregnant—in which case
they didn't have to go on the transport. Or I said people
had temperatures of 39.8 or 40.2 degrees Centigrade
(103 to 104 degrees Fahrenheit) so that they too were
transportunfähig, as the Germans called it. I had to sub-
mit my list to Spanier, the head doctor, and to begin
with he followed my advice.

How he came to suspect that something was being
"tried on" I don't know. Once, when I had once again
managed to declare a number of people unfit for transportation on the grounds of high temperature, he sent a
male nurse, a *Sanitäter*, in my tracks, who took all their
temperatures again, and they all turned out to be
normal or even less. I was then called up before
Spanier, who showed me my list and the nurse's. And
he said, "Look, Cohen, you've already done this several
times and now you've been caught out at it. Do it once
more, and you and your family will be put on a transport."

Look, when I think about this now, later on, I see
that I ought to have said to him there and then, "All
right, but in that case I'm not doing this work any
longer. You'll have to take someone else in my place

and put me on a transport." I didn't find the courage to. After this warning, I gave more or less honest medical reports. Of course there were those I was still able to let slip through—anyone can make a mistake—but I dropped the deliberate intention with which I had gone to work on so many nights before.

It wasn't only in this case but in many another too that I saw that man is an egoist. Someone who thinks only of his own safety. The Germans had a cunning system, and the more I have read about it, the clearer it has become to me that it *was* a system. They employed it everywhere they were in power, in the ghettos, in Poland, in Amsterdam, everywhere. They would say to a few people, "No, you don't have to go on a transport, you'll get a suspension [a *Sperr* was their word for it] but, of course, the others *do* have to go on a transport, and you'll have to help with that." So that's what I did. I don't want to say anything at all about other people, for I haven't the right to. But I myself collaborated. I was "honest" (between inverted commas), as far as I could be. I was obedient and did the job I had to do in a completely, yes, "honest" way. That wasn't very nice of me; it wasn't decent, and it wasn't courageous. It is a fact, one of the facts, of which I am ashamed. I definitely wasn't extra mean, but—and this probably applies to everyone who came out of the concentration camps alive—I'm tarred. I allowed my own interests to prevail over the general good, or over an honest attitude in my life, based on principles.

For I really did have a great deal of influence in Westerbork. I had become a "prominent" person, and as a result I could keep people I wanted to off the transports—my family, for instance. I was able to protect my parents-in-law, who had arrived in Westerbork in April, in this way, as long as I was "in power," so to say. I was able to protect an uncle and aunt of mine. A cousin of mine was in the OD, this was the *Ordedienst,* a sort of Jewish police force, and every Sunday or Monday he would come to me and say, "Elie, father's and mother's names are down on the transport list, what are we going to do about it?"

"In that case," I would say, "we'll have to admit them to hospital."

I could exert an influence on the doctor in charge of hospital admissions, and through this chap one or the other of the two was admitted to hospital, which meant that the other one was "barred" from going on a transport as well. It even happened that I once had to get them in and out of the hospital twice over. To begin with, it was said that everyone in the hospital was "barred," and so the husband was admitted. Then my cousin came along and said, "No, the hospital isn't "barred" after all—they must be got out again."

So I went again to the admissions doctor, or rather, to the discharge doctor this time, and said, "That uncle of mine must come out."

That was on a Monday, and that same afternoon my cousin came back again and said, "I was mistaken. The hospital is 'barred' after all."

And so off I went again to the admissions doctor and deposited my uncle in hospital once more. I had the power to do that, you see.

I'm being a bit incoherent, because the rest of it is all so emotional. Since the Germans had given me the feeling I was completely protected by that red stamp of theirs, *and* because I was always the doctor who could examine the people arriving on the incoming transports, if they needed it, I saw that I could exert no influence at all for those who came to Westerbork with an S against their names—the punishment cases, that is to say. An S-case was inevitably sent on to Auschwitz—that was how it was—unless he had very important connections, which was the position in my own case. For my attempt to escape from Holland meant that I had arrived at Westerbork in December 1942, as an S-case myself.

My sister was married and had been a nurse in the town of Apeldoorn, having left there in fairly good time to become a nurse in the Dutch-Israelite Hospital in Amsterdam. And since I saw that I could do nothing for all these people who were S-cases (who had gone underground but been found out), I got that cousin of mine, who worked with the OD and so had to go to Amsterdam now and then, to tell my sister not to go into hiding, for in that case I should be utterly powerless to help her, should she be caught and arrive in Westerbork as an S-case.

And this turned out to be such horrifically wrong advice. When she did, in fact, arrive in Westerbork with her husband, my sister said to me, "I've taken your advice, but I was rather well protected in Amsterdam. For even during the big roundups of Jews I used to walk about without wearing my Jewish star, because I don't look a bit like a Jewess, and they have always taken me for an Aryan woman. I've never had any problem at all. But you have made me so afraid, and so here I am. And now, what are you going to do for me?"

I was able to do a little. I was able to keep her off the transports a few times. A few times, I say. For the day came when my authority was reduced to naught.

I don't know how familiar people are with those houses in Westerbork. There was a small back room in them in which four people slept and a small front room where two families slept. That's to say, in our house, in our front room, six people slept, with four in the back room. In that front room we lived with a German Jewish couple, a doctor I knew from Groningen. He was a typical Prussian. Everything had to be in a special place, and if it wasn't in its place, he got angry. Once my wife failed to put something in its proper place and he raised hell about it. Although we were Zionists and didn't, as a matter of principle, want to recognize any difference between German Jews, American Jews, or Dutch Jews, my wife said to him all the same, "You're a typically German Jew. Everything has to be organized for you. Otherwise you get into a panic."

This was told to Spanier, and one day I was sum-

Collection point for Jews in Amsterdam.

Departure of Jews from Amsterdam to Westerbork.

Entraining at Westerbork.

Loading cattle cars for Auschwitz.

moned into his presence, and he said to me, "All Jews are the same. There's no difference between them. You say you are a Zionist, but that's not true, because you've lumped all the German Jews together. You've insulted them. Your wife has said this and that to so-and-so. From this moment on, my protection of you no longer applies."

He acted pretty speedily too. There was an end to the "Regulars List" with the red stamp and for the very first time I failed to get a *Zettel*, which was a slip of paper saying I was free to move about the camp on the day a transport was leaving. I had always had that previously, when I was a transport doctor, that is to say, the doctor who could, and was allowed to, do something still for the departing transports. In the middle of the night, the notorious chit accordingly arrived for me, reading: "On the orders of the *Obersturm-führer:* You must take into account [this was the impressive language they used] that tonight you will be leaving by transport." And it was a fact: at five o'clock in the morning I received notice that I was going on the transport.

That guilt feeling. Is it a guilt feeling? You do such things, like the advice I gave my sister, thinking you are acting for the best. And when it turns out you have given the wrong advice, have guessed wrong, you naturally ask yourself: Would she (my sister) still be alive, if I hadn't given her that advice? That bothers me, and naturally I often find I'm wrestling with this problem. Because it's an emotional feeling of guilt you can't reason away, of course. They say that twenty thousand went underground and that ten thousand of them saved their lives that way. And then, of course, you say to yourself: she might just as well have been one of those ten thousand. But you're still left with the problem. There was *something* I could do. This was in connection with the incoming transports, among which there were friends of mine, and then their parents too. And these people would come to me and say, "If my father arrives tonight, or if my mother arrives tonight, can you do something for them?" Then, when the contingent had come into the registration hall and they had all been registered and so arrived in my cubicle, I could say, "This man is sick. He must be admitted to hospital immediately." This would save them from having to take the road to the shower bath, or to Lippmann Rosenthal, the Jewish bank where they had to leave all their money and silver and so on; and save them from other things too I can't recall at the moment. And especially arriving in those overcrowded barrack huts— a thing which always came as a shock to the people coming from their comfortable homes in the fashionable residential quarter of south Amsterdam. And they weren't even the wealthy people; the less well-to-do had had good homes too, if you compared them with Westerbork.

5

Life at Westerbork

ONE THING I WAS NOT—and I'd like to make that clear. I wasn't corrupt. I was offered plenty. Women even offered themselves to me. I'm no saint—but I never fell for that. I never declared people unfit to go on one of the transports in return for money or other things. That standard I did, evidently, maintain in Westerbork. And that was an important standard, for there was, of course, a good deal of corruption, and there were plenty of dealings in money and diamonds and I don't know what. But no, I didn't descend as low as that.

But now comes this crazy thing. The crazy thing that was actually going on within me through the whole of the war—that you anticipated certain measures. The Germans were here, in the Netherlands, after all, and they *were* the bosses here, after all. Being moved out of your doctor's practice—it wasn't at all pleasant, of course, but you'd *expected* it. You went to live in a house, and there certain restrictions were placed upon you: you weren't allowed out in the street after a certain hour; you weren't allowed a bike, an automobile; weren't allowed to board a bus or streetcar anymore.

These were all things which tallied with what you had expected. And that's why I wasn't all that scared when I was put on the transport to leave Westerbork. I had expected that. We said to one another too, "That's what you're in Westerbork for—to be put on a transport. Not to stay here. And if you've stayed here for some time and it hasn't been too bad, that's something to be thankful for."

I did not know absolutely for sure that it would be worse elsewhere. But in the Netherlands, you knew what you had, and you expected it to be something strange, something not so good in another place.

I remember how once, on one of the mornings when a transport was leaving, a Tuesday morning, two OD workers brought a tiny woman from the hospital to the train. A little old woman of ninety-five. And those OD men said to me, "Just look at this, doctor. Ninety-five years old. Labor Supply. Can you believe it?"

Naturally, there was always something that made us shudder, but then the indestructible optimism and the indestructible will to live people had came to the surface again. They drove back their fear and thought: "Oh well, it won't be so good for the old folk but the young ones . . . well, they'll have to work, but it won't turn out so bad."

We fooled one another the whole time. Even in those cattle trucks which took us to Auschwitz. I was sitting in that train with my wife, my little boy, and my parents-in-law, who'd lost the protection they'd enjoyed when my "regulars list" collapsed. Oh yes, it was a nasty journey. No one knew where he was going to and everyone was scared. We ate practically nothing, although we had taken some food with us. I was talking with my wife and at one point she said, "You look just as you did when we went to Amsterdam from Groningen after being arrested. Are you expecting something terrible like that then?" What could I say? I didn't know what I was expecting. Nothing pleasant, but nothing bad either.

A few more words about Westerbork. I have read a lot about life being so hard there, so frightfully difficult a life. But that wasn't what I experienced there. Naturally, it all came as a terrible shock to people to land up out of their homes in those huts. You were on the bottom rung of the ladder there. You were "material for transportation." We were always tensed up too. We knew that every Tuesday another transport would be leaving. And if there wasn't enough "transport material" —to use that rotten expression—we only hoped a good transport would arrive, for God's sake, from Amsterdam on Friday evening. By which we could protect our own people, whom we wanted to protect. For those new people arrived in Westerbork completely at a loss. They didn't know the ropes. They didn't know either that there were still some ways out. For instance, that they could try to show they were indeed married to Aryans or had indeed had Aryan grandparents, or something else. Those people usually didn't have time to try to get off the next transport to Auschwitz.

I once described the journey from Westerbork to

Auschwitz in the Amsterdam daily, *Het Algemeen Handelsblad.* And I received a very remarkable reaction from a well-known doctor in Amsterdam. After reading my article, he said, "I'm extremely grateful to you for this article. Until I read it I had always lived in uncertainty and had worried about the feelings my mother must have had when she was over eighty and went to Auschwitz. Now that you have stated it so clearly and made it seem plausible to me that 'the train' did not know what would happen in Auschwitz, you have given me greater peace of mind and I have gotten rid of a lot of unpleasant feelings as a result."

What was our life like there, in Westerbork? It sounds crazy, of course, but you went out to those incoming transports—they usually arrived at eleven or twelve o'clock—as though going to an outing. You went and dressed carefully. You shaved before you went, and you spoke to the other people who were going out to the train, with whom you had gradually come to be on friendly terms. It was like going out. What arrived— that didn't affect you. You were cheerful. You enjoyed yourself. And after that you did your work. And then, when I was standing in the small cubicle where I worked—in a white jacket, of course: there always had to be status—you would suddenly hear *"Achtung!"* ring through the hall, and then the *Obersturmführer* came in person to take a look at "his" Jews. Then he would come to me too and ask if everything was going all right. I would then stand at attention, very stiff, the same probably as every soldier has stood at attention, and say, *"Jawohl, Herr Obersturmführer. Nein, Herr Obersturmführer."*

Afterward we would go calmly to one or another and drink a cup of tea or a cup of coffee. Whether it was a form of self-protection (that's what it will have been) . . . but it was also because we knew no facts . . . you weren't so terribly affected. You did that work and you were glad that you had gotten on so far in Westerbork, that you no longer needed to creep around the camp so abjectly and so scared. Although my present wife often says that I am not judging the matter honestly, Westerbork is not a horror to me. I had come from Amersfoort, and *that* was awful. That was a concentration camp. But Westerbork, where I was met by my wife and came to live in a small house, where there was enough to eat, where parcels arrived—I was never able to look on that as something terrible. Especially because, as a Jew, you enjoyed more freedom inside Westerbork than outside it. During the week you were allowed to walk about the camp in the evenings and you didn't have to be scared, because some SS man might suddenly come up to you.

The curse of Westerbork was always that transport train, of course. That train . . . if it happened to be a bit late—it usually arrived on a Monday, usually about twelve o'clock—and if it hadn't arrived by twelve o'clock, or by one, or by two o'clock, people would begin to hope: there *isn't* any train this week and there isn't going to be one either. But once it was there a

shudder would go through the whole camp and everyone in danger of being transported on it would scurry
from the one to the other, asking, "Can't you do something for me? Who can help me? Will *you* do something for me?" It was just like a beehive until nine
o'clock in the evening, until *Lagersperre*—Lights Out.

When I myself at last got my notice, I reacted to it
with resignation, with absolute resignation. I did just
call in at the clinic and ask a colleague, a German
Jewish doctor, whether he could do anything about it
for me. But he said, "You know perfectly well I can't.
There's no doing anything about an order from the
Obersturmführer. That hasn't come from Records, that's
come from the *Obersturmführer* personally."

Just one little joke. A fortnight ago I was taking part
in an open discussion, and Professor Speijer was taking
part too. I said to him, "Nico, you, I believe, were put
'on transport' a good twenty times. When you were
on one, had you any idea at all what lay beyond Westerbork?" And he replied, "No, I can prove it too. Van der
Hal came from the camp at Vught and went to Auschwitz via Westerbork. I went to him and saw that he had
only one suit. I had two. And I went back to my room,
took a suit, and went to Isaac and said, "Look, Izzy,
this is a very good suit. I'm giving it you because you're
going on, but I have an important request. When you
return, I must have it back, otherwise I'll be without a
suit myself."

Well, proof . . . anyway, at least such things are

indications that we *really* didn't know. People say, of course, that we repressed it, but I'd never heard a thing. And I'll even go so far as to say that if we *had* heard about it, we shouldn't have believed it. It is something which lies completely beyond one's powers of imagination. One *can't* believe it.

Westerbork. Life there was agreeable. When the transport had left, on a Tuesday morning, I went to the bathhouse (I was privileged), took a shower, went to my small room, and slept for an hour. And in the evening we went out. Then Willy Rosen would perform, with the cabaret of the *prominenten*—that is, well-known performers. There was a good orchestra under the direction of Sal Dwinger and someone else. In short, we were "out for the evening." And the next transport was not until another week's time, and what might not happen in a week? Mussolini had been ousted once, and who was to say what might not happen in Germany? A week, a week, a week was so long. But the closer that Tuesday came, the more things began to buzz like a beehive, an ant heap. Everyone was moving about, just to try to make good friends with the people who pulled the strings there.

For who compiled the list of names for the transports? I never knew exactly, of course, what orders were given. I can visualize Gemmeker saying to Schlesinger, "There's got to be a transport of three thousand on Tuesday." And that was then passed on to the "Writing Room"—they were Jews in there. Then someone sat at the box with all our cards in it, and it was

he really who made up the contingent for transportation. That office decided who went and who didn't.
Gemmeker had no hand in that. Yes, once—when a few
people tried to escape, he said, "Now an extra ten will
go on the transport." As punishment. But that was one
of the rare occasions that he interfered with the transports. He said how many and the Jews did the rest.

And this is really the way things went everywhere.
If you read about the Warsaw ghetto, of the ghetto at
Lodz, everywhere there were the "Jewish Elders" and
the "Jewish Council," and it was they who did the work.
In Auschwitz, later on, it was the same too. But the SS
were far more active there. Oh, you felt good in Westerbork. You felt a cut above the "plebs." But that was
only possible because I was a doctor—that is the red
thread you can trace through all my war years. That
being a doctor—I've said so before—it was an enormous
advantage to me, an enormous shield.

Westerbork. It was friendly. You paid one another
visits. You made dates. Whoring went on there, flirting,
drinking. There was something of everything, just as in
ordinary life. It was only once a week that a crazy train
like that came along, and then that had to carry off so
many Jews. Every list of exemptions came to nothing
(*platzte*—exploded—we called it) sooner or later, and
you simply accepted it. But it just isn't true that you
let it get you down for long. At least, not as far as I was
concerned. For afterward life went on as usual again.

6

Transport to Auschwitz

So my little boy had been operated on for his ear, and in the cattle truck on that train there was a peephole. He was very keen on peering through it, to see the countryside gliding past. But I kept calling him away, because, in fact, I was dead scared he might get that otitis again. That, too, is proof I didn't know, hadn't the faintest idea, what went on there, farther on, in Auschwitz. I did not know. And you can blame yourself for that afterward, but you can't base your life on things you might have heard rumored now and then. They fooled me, they fooled me very badly indeed. Of course, I had formed some sort of idea of Auschwitz. I always imagined it was the same as what I had heard about Vught. A camp for Jews, where you had to work (there was a diamond industry in Vught; Philips, the radio firm, worked there, and other industries too). And then there was also a concentration camp. That was my very simple conception of Auschwitz: a central camp for Jews, and the people who went there as S-cases, punishment cases, that's to say, well, they landed up in the concentration camp. And that wasn't so nice.

But by the time we went to Auschwitz I was no longer an S-case. I'd asked a friend who was in the Records Office at Westerbork about that. He took a look to see if there was still an S on my card. There was, and so he took the card out and substituted another without an S on it. I considered that terribly important.

The atmosphere in that train. Difficult to describe. One man was put in charge as the *Wagonführer*. All these *Wagonführer*s had to report to the *Obersturm-führer* some time before we left. Ours came back and said, "Boys, I've been appointed *Wagonführer*, and I've been told that if as much as one of you escapes, it'll mean my death. Don't make it difficult for me, and let's try to make the best of it. Don't try to escape, or it'll cost me my life." It was once more an appeal to our solidarity. Everyone thought: Ought you to escape when it can cost that man his life? All a swindle, for no one checked the list later on. They didn't count the people either. They knew the number in Westerbork, but on arrival in Auschwitz we weren't counted. So you could, in fact, have escaped without it being noticed.

I wouldn't have done so, no. I didn't expect so much of people. Later on I often asked men who worked in the resistance movement a question. When they told me they had blown up railroad lines and been present at the dropping of arms, I'd ask them, "Why then, in the name of God, didn't you destroy the line to Wester-bork? Why didn't you once disrupt that junction in

Ommen on the way to it, so that the transports couldn't have gotten through for a few weeks, or even just for one day?" I do have an explanation for this. When did the resistance get properly under way in Holland? It was in 1943, probably not until the end of 1943. And I've read somewhere—I no longer know where—that 30 per cent of the Jews had already been taken away by January 1, 1943. And with those big roundups in July, August, and September, probably more than half of them had already left. So by the time the resistance movement had become a force the Germans had to reckon with, most of the Jews would have already left the country. Of course, they could still have tried it, but there's no doubt they didn't. Oh, it's so easy to make reproaches. And I'm no hero either. I've a deep respect for what those fellows did. But this . . . oh, well, don't let's say unpleasant things about it, for there's absolutely no point in that. They didn't see it, and they didn't know. The resistance movement in Holland was too late in getting going, and I believe that is one of the reasons.

That train. Yes, the mood on it was gloomy. No doubt about that. People still got embarrassed. There was a bin in that cattle truck and you had to relieve yourself into it. We fixed a small curtain round it so that there was at least some sort of privacy. Now and again the train stopped, and the SS men then started organizing things in their special fashion.

"Hand in all your watches," they said. "And all your gold rings."

By chance I had nothing with me. I'd handed over what I had to someone else, who was to hand it over to someone else too, in his turn. And that's what happened. After the war, I got back my fountain pen and my pencil and my watch and gold rings. Those SS types were after money too. "It'll be taken off you, anyway," they said. "So why not give it to us?" They'll have made a tidy haul.

And every time we halted there was a cordon of SS men round the train. We could see that through that peephole. The doors were practically never opened. Oh, it was only for two days, and everyone sat there, sunk deep in his private thoughts. I was sitting in that train with my parents-in-law, and you knew . . . well, knew . . . actually, you *knew* nothing—but you were very much afraid it meant the end for them.

I said that my father was a waiter. He and my mother had been taken to Auschwitz in December 1942. And at a certain moment my wife said to me, "Well, you never know, perhaps we shall see your father there, serving in the bar at Auschwitz." I mean, we thought: Westerbork is simply being transferred to Auschwitz and that it'll be just the same there as it was in Westerbork. You have to work a bit, the one rather harder than the other.

When she had left for Auschwitz, my mother had left a letter behind for me in Westerbork. I arrived there only later. I read that letter. Lost it too, which is a great pity. We could not visualize it. The Polish Jews will have known much more, of course. In the first place, they were far more used to anti-Semitism than we were. In the second place, they had already contributed their share to the labor squads, the *Einsatzcommandos*, out of which the Jews were taken and every manjack of them machine-gunned. Then, in Poland, there was Chelmno. And there was Belzec too, and Sobibor—all notorious extermination camps. And that hadn't all remained a secret. There is still in existence a letter from some rabbi, who wrote to another rabbi: "What goes on in Chelmno defies all description. The Jews are being murdered there the whole time."

In Poland, of course, the rumors were stronger. Treblinka lay a good way off from Warsaw, yet wasn't so very far. I read somewhere that someone noted down the numbers of the train wagons and checked when they came back empty; in this way he worked out that the camp must be so many hours from Warsaw. I've also read that someone once escaped from Treblinka and got to the ghetto in Warsaw and told them about it there. But even in Warsaw they weren't inclined to believe it. At least, not all of it. And one can understand that as well, once you inquire into when the resistance began in Warsaw. That was in 1943, and by then there was only 10 per cent of the entire Jewish population left. The remainder certainly didn't believe it all.

And all at once the train stopped. September the sixteenth, nineteen hundred and forty-three. And where are we, eh? Where are we? That train had gone

back to Westerbork from Auschwitz a few times. And
when it arrived in Westerbork it was cleaned out. And
then little notes were discovered from people who had
written, "We're about to get out here." "We can see
camps." "We can see people in striped uniforms." This
didn't tell us much, of course, for they couldn't hide
away a description of what happened afterward in that
train.

We were slung out pretty quickly. No, "Slung out"
is an exaggeration, but we had to get out very smartly.
Luggage you had to leave behind—oh, well, everyone
knows that—and then my wife fainted. There was some
muddy water lying there and I moistened her wrists
with it. I still don't know—of course, I don't—*why* she
fainted. An SS guard came up and said something such
as, "Calm down a bit. It's nothing very special." Right.
The lot of us were split up, the cocks separated from
the hens. My wife, my little boy, and my mother-in-law
went and stood in one row, and the men in another row.
Then the row of men was divided up again.

I went and stood next to my father-in-law. I thought
that maybe I could help him. He was an old man, over
seventy, and I was still only in my thirties. Until suddenly—and here it comes again . . . I don't know
whether you believe in God. I don't believe in God, but
there are things which make you think: Is there, after
all, some pattern in this life? If I had not had a coronary a few years ago, I should have gone on plugging
away in my practice as a general practitioner and
should never have done the work I am doing now and

Entrance to Auschwitz.

The label reads:
"POISON GAS!
Store in a cool, dry place.
Keep from the sun and open
flame. To be opened and used
only by experienced
personnel."

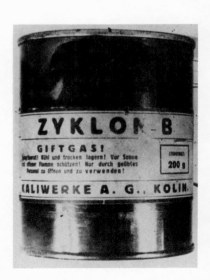

Labor squad in action near Duneburg, November 1941.

Prisoners liberated by Patton's
Third Army at Ebensee, Austria,
May 6, 1945.

am so happy in, because I feel it is what I really ought
to be doing. And then I should have felt bitter about it.
Then others would have done this work, who, to my
way of thinking, had less right to it. Of course, I'm
not *grateful* I had a coronary, but it has meant that my
life has taken a certain turn, which at the moment
makes me feel I really am doing something worthwhile.

So, as I said, I was standing next to my father-in-
law, and that's what made me just say something about
Providence. Then, suddenly, they called out, "Doctors,
step forward!" Just imagine that I had not heard those
words—it could have happened, of course. If I had
been standing a little farther up or had been talking at
that particular moment, or . . . well, if I just hadn't
heard them. But I *did* hear them. We reported to some
SS man or other and he said, "You must stand over
there." Okay. We were still in the dark. No, they didn't
ask me if I could prove I was a doctor. I had papers
with me, but they didn't ask to see them. They simply
took your word for it. That is why many a one who
wasn't a doctor said he was. I had to find that out to my
cost, but I'll be coming back to that. Then the trucks
arrived and women got into them. And the last I saw
of one of those trucks was my wife, and my child, and
my mother-in-law. We waved to one another and didn't
act at all alarmed, not in the least panicky. Didn't think:
this is our last adieu. No, nothing of that kind. You
simply waved. I thought, Oh, well, we'll be seeing each
other again soon. How, I didn't know, but all the same:
we'll be seeing each other again soon. Okay, my mother-

in-law was old, and my little boy was four by then, and I saw nothing special at all in their going off in that truck.

We walked our way to Auschwitz. You saw people walking about in striped suits, the labor squads, and I thought, There you are, you see—I was right. Those will be the punishment cases and they have to work here. And then we arrived in Auschwitz, where we were lined up between two blocks. A colleague of mine, married to a distant cousin, came walking up, and he was in a striped uniform. He had also been brought to Auschwitz as an S-case. You see? It was just as well that that S had been removed from my card. Well, we had to undress and go under the shower. Didn't think for a moment that it might *not* be water that came out of that shower! That's terribly important, eh? Didn't think of it for one second.

Okay, we came out of that shower bath and had to wait outside. Now, I'd rescued my stethoscope and my doctor's diploma. I pushed the diploma into my wrap and was holding my stethoscope in my hand. Then there was another inspection, and, oh well, they took that away too. We were pretty soon disillusioned: we had to wear the same striped uniforms and were allocated to some place in Auschwitz.

Leen Sanders came up to us. He was a professional boxer at the time and now lives in America. And he told us what happened in Auschwitz. That was, of course, an incredible . . . well, it was a blow. To hear your family had been gassed. And the strange thing is:

you believed it right away. You believed it right away. So it couldn't have come entirely as a surprise to you. You didn't say, "Oh, that can't be true!" No, no, you *believed* it.

Then we were called to assemble again, and again they shouted out, "All doctors step forward!" Four men did. Eddie de Wind and I, a young fellow called Zwarenstein or something like that—he's living in Brussels now—and a fourth one whose name I can no longer recall. Zwarenstein wasn't a doctor at all. (I had a word with him again only a year ago.) They needed three doctors, so one had to drop out. I was that one.

We were taken to Buna, where the synthetic rubber was made for the IG-Farben concern. By now I had heard about that gas chamber and I was scared. And so I said to everyone I took to be someone of importance, "I'm a doctor, and I'd like to be put to work as one." And I said this too to the senior man of our tent—for we slept in tents there. And the next day this man said to me, "You must go along to the camp doctor then." And to him I went. They tested me for my medical qualifications. That's to say, I had to undress and walk to and fro.

Then that doctor said, "Are you lame?"

"Not that I know of," I replied.

"Well, in that case, just walk up and down again."

And this time I must have walked properly, for he said I should be "appointed"—that's what they called it: *eingesetzt*—as a nurse or something. Not even, I think, as a doctor.

When, the following morning, the men had to line

up to go off to the labor squads, I was allowed to stay
behind in the tent. This signified an enormous protection. In the evenings the other lads came back and
said it had been frightful. Bernard Koster—another one
I'd met in Amersfoort—said right away, "I don't know
whether I'll be able to keep it up."

I wanted to keep it up. I had heard that my wife
and my little boy were no longer alive. But the maddest
thing of all is that you go on fighting. You go on fighting. There will undoubtedly have been those who
didn't, once they knew. But I did. Nor did I see any
others giving in. Everyone went on fighting again.
When they had called out that "All doctors step forward!" I had run as quickly as the next man to get
there. For I had remembered exactly *that* from the
camp at Amersfoort: *if* there was any chance at all of
saving myself, it would have to be via my profession.
Because I didn't know if I should be able to keep up
that heavy physical labor. That will to live, that forcing
yourself to carry on, that survives. It just happens to be
like that. Of course, you got into a state of shock, and
the shock was bigger for one man than for another . . .
oh, well, I don't know, and I can't really explain it very
clearly. I wanted to go on living. It isn't a noble attitude
maybe. But it's true. That's how it is. I did my best,
just that.

I was taken back to Auschwitz again, in a kind of
medical van. There were a few other chaps too, and
they didn't look in any too good condition, and that's
why I kept on saying, "Yes, I mustn't go to the gas

chamber. I must go to work." Those chaps thought me
completely crazy, I imagine. And when we got out in
Auschwitz and had to go into some "block," I said it
again to the senior man in that block. He said, in German: "You've got a screw loose, man!" He was right
too, of course.

Okay. I landed up in a sick block, and I could have
lost my life again there. In that block—it was Block 9—
I was allotted to work on the ambulance. And there,
there was Erwin Valentin, a German surgeon and an
exceptionally kind chap. And after some days he said
to me, "I say, Cohen, do you think you're here to con-
valesce?"

"No," I said, "that hadn't occurred to me for a
second."

"But don't you hear it then, every time they call out
'Kettle Duty!'?" he asked.

"Yes, I hear it," I said.

"But that means you've got to go and carry the
kettles with the soup and the tea."

"Oh, I didn't know that," I said.

So I went and lined up for that too and began to
haul kettles about.

I don't know exactly how it happened, but a couple
of days later a barrel full of soup toppled over and it
was my fault. Well, that's quite a thing to happen in a
block like that. They were terribly mad with me. But
nothing happened—I was allowed to go on working in
peace. And then, as though the devil was playing a

game with me, the next day it happened again. Then
the man in charge of the food gave me a terrific bawl-
ing-out. And he was quite right to do so, too, because
it amounted to a disaster. The block superior said to
me, "You know, I really ought to send you back into the
camp and then you'll just have to work in the ordinary
labor squads. But I'll give you one more chance. You'll
be coming into the Lunatics' Room."

That's to say, there was one room in the block full
of non-Jewish psychotic cases and lunatics, Poles. Now
and then a bunch of Jewish Mussulmen would arrive,
but they were got rid of again. Mussulmen are people
who are . . . well, very, very lean, who are very
slow in their reactions, walk bent over forward, slow,
moving about like ghosts, who have given up the strug-
gle to keep alive. They weigh only about eighty pounds
and lose a lot of weight. They were always being
selected for the gas chamber, but I'll talk about that in
a minute or two.

So I landed up in the Lunatics' Ward, and there it
was a Jewish Czech doctor who saved my life. (He
committed suicide a few years ago. I visited him just
once in Czechoslovakia, and he came to Holland once,
too.) For, you see, no one wanted to carry those soup
kettles with me anymore. That fellow doesn't know how
to carry the kettles properly, and if he tips another over,
I'll be in for it too, was what they all thought. I don't
know what it was, but at a certain moment I just
couldn't do it anymore. I could feel the thing slipping
out of my grasp. There were others who felt the same

thing, but they had thought up some trick. They took a strap and tied it round the handles. But I hadn't got that far. It always had to be done quickly, at the double. And they were big soup kettles, real vats. It was a thing you had to learn the knack of.

Well, this Czech doctor then said to me, "I'll carry those kettles with you, and then we'll see to it that you learn the knack too."

He did the job with me for a week, and then it went all right, and I had no more difficulties in this respect.

I wasn't simply the doctor in the Lunatics' Room in Block 9 but also had the magnificent job of *Scheisshausmeister*—Master of the Bog. That's to say, it was my duty to see that the w.c.s and urinals were kept spotlessly clean. So it was a combined task. As room doctor, you immediately had a better time of it. You got the good food, and your portions were never the smallest. The work wasn't so terribly interesting, because there were no medicines. If the lunatics became too troublesome, you shoved them into a strait jacket.

Something very nasty happened once. In the middle of the night a lunatic escaped from the room and went into the camp. The next day the block superior was summoned to appear before the SS commander. When he came back he told the block doctor that from that night onward it was never to happen again, a lunatic entering the camp. The block doctor passed the message on to the room superior, and the room superior passed it on to me. And I had no one to pass it on to.

So I was faced with this problem. I went to a man for whom I felt the greatest respect, to Valentin, and told him from that night on it had to be quiet in our block.

"Or else?" he inquired.

"Or else we'll all be for the gas chamber," I said.

"Well," he said, "*du dumme Holländer*, what must you do then?"

"No, I can't do that," I said.

The way he went for me!

"Still keeping to those principles of yours! Sacrificing six hundred people for one lunatic! Do you dare to now?"

"No," I said.

"All right then," he said. "In that case, I'll help you. Bring him along here."

And that's what I did.

We had a large supply of insulin—I don't know how we got hold of it—and he gave that man (he did or I did, I wouldn't even dare say which of us it was at the moment) two hundred units of insulin. And from then on it was quiet in our block.

On that occasion I . . . yes, I infringed the ethical rule that one is a doctor not to murder people, but to try to keep them alive, to try to cure them, help them. And . . . it's always the first step that counts. For a few weeks later, it happened again. But by that time I had far fewer moral scruples about going upstairs again and saying to Valentin, "Same old thing. We'll have to do it again."

And we did too, and that man died as well.

It was quite simple, of course, for you just filled in something on the deceased's cards. Pneumonia . . . anything you liked. For it was all a farce in that room. I kept a very neat chart for each patient, showing his temperature and even the medicines we were giving him. Or were *not* giving him rather, even though they were entered on his chart.

Once every two weeks the camp doctor arrived. It was always announced in advance. *Heute Kommission* —inspection today. That meant the whole block had to shine like a new penny. Then I would apply myself with great devotion to my lavatories. I sprinkled liberal doses of chloride of lime in them. Hardly were you inside than your eyes began to water. If they said anything about that, I thought to myself: it's better that your eyes smart than that I get bawled out. I would stand on guard to make sure no one went to the w.c. And then one of the big bugs would go anyway, and say, "*Scheisse* to you!" if I made any remark about it. Then off I'd go to that pot again, clean it, and down went another load of lime. Well then, at last the *Kommission* arrived. Dr. Klein, a Rumanian doctor—he was condemned at the Bergen Belsen trial and hanged— came in with his SDG, that meant *Sanitäts Dienst Grad* or something of the kind, a German subordinate, say, a German medical orderly. All very friendly. The only thing missing was that he didn't address me as a colleague and say, "*Guten Morgen, Herr Kollege!*" but merely, "*Guten Morgen.*"

And then I fetched the people—the Jews only—out

of their beds and picked up their charts. And he would
say to me, "What's wrong with this man?" Well now,
the one was suffering from general debility, another
had bronchitis, another pneumonia. But all of them
were living skeletons, living corpses. I gave him their
names and then he asked, "How long do you think it
will be before this man is fit for work again?" And in
one case I might say three weeks and in another four.
And then he would take the chart out of my hands,
glance at it, and hand it over to the SS man at his side.
Now and then he would also return a chart to me. But
the first time all this happened I wasn't fully aware of
everything it signified.

I've already said that Klein was very polite, and he
would also inquire with interest whether I still had
medicines, or what I wished to do in some particular
case, whether the men did any gymnastics, whether
they got sufficient physical exercise. The man really was
exceptionally willing, and exceptionally friendly, you'd
say, in carrying out his deadly task. The people whose
charts he had handed to the SS man were collected in
army trucks. Even today I can't drive behind an army
truck without . . . without seeing it all before me
again. Those people left the block—in their nightshirts
—and landed up in that truck, and then Levi, the room
superior said, "Another load for the gas chamber."

And then I suddenly began to weep. I can still see
it. We had a small screened-off corner belonging to the
room superior, where we had our meals, being the
"leaders" of that room. "But it's so inhuman," I said.
"You just can't do a thing like that."

Oh, I was beside myself the first time. But, well, you get over it.

Two weeks later it happened all over again. Again I told Dr. Klein the men's names, and again he handed the charts to the SS man or back to me. And the Germans never said these people were being sent to their death. The Germans always had such fine names for things like that. In this case it was "SB"—*Sonderbehandlung*—special treatment. And special treatment meant gas. And that's the way people went who'd lain longer in that room too. The psychotics were left there. *They* didn't go into the gas chamber, *they* were Aryans. Only the Jews, who simply needed two, say, three months of good food and rest to become normal people again. *They* went.

7

The Last Selection at Auschwitz

HAVE I TOLD YOU about the last selection in Auschwitz?
The last selection in Auschwitz was at the beginning
of October 1944. Then thousands went into the gas
chamber. The selection of the people in the camp
proper (those in the labor squads, that is) was very
simple. *Mijnheer* Klein—Dr. Klein, that's to say—had
the people trek past him. He had a dog with him and a
nice little woman with whom he was cheerily chatting
away. He stroked his dog, and now and then he pulled
one man out. Then he went on chatting and gave his
dog another stroke.

We had "selection" in the sick block too. I had been
promoted—that meant I had adapted myself still further. I was now the room doctor for people who were
really sick. And I had an assistant. In another room lay
a Dutch professor. I would visit him several times a day
and on one occasion he said to me, "D'you know,
Cohen, what makes me happiest of all?"

"No, professor."

"That my son is in the resistance. I'm proud of that."
(He didn't know, of course, that his son had been dead
a long time.)

Every time the inspection came round, we began to
gamble. One time we'd say, "Now, everyone we mark
down as sick for more than two weeks, of course, will
go to the gas chamber." Or: one week, or three weeks.
Well, we gambled on three weeks. That's to say, anyone who had been registered sick for *more* than three
weeks would go "into the gas."

So I went to the doctor of the room where the professor was lying and asked him what he was betting on.

"Well," he said, "last time it was three weeks."

"Okay," I said. "Will you put him down as three
weeks then."

And so the camp doctor was told he was a three-
week case, with the addition that he'd be fit for work
again in three weeks' time. But that time the limit was
fixed at two weeks, and everyone who had been registered sick for more than two weeks went to the gas
chamber.

The day the gassing was to take place I went to the
professor, who said to me, "Cohen, I've a very big favor
to ask you. Would you do it?"

"I don't know what you mean, professor," I said.

"Will you see to it that I'm given enough narcotics
to make sure I'm no longer conscious when I go into
the gas chamber?"

I didn't do it. I didn't do it. Images that haunt you.
That day was a very anxious day for me altogether, for

that matter. Death touched my arm twice that day.

One time I saw a young boy of about sixteen kneeling in front of a high-ranking SS man, his hands raised and imploring him, "*Mijnheer* SS man, I can work. I'm willing to work. Don't send me to the gas chamber." The SS man smiled and turned away. There were patients in the room who were unable to walk unaided. My assistant and I then made a chair with our arms and carried them downstairs. But the first time we left that block there was an SS guard standing counting at the exit: "eleven, twelve, thirteen . . ." I can still hear those numbers. And we put a man in the truck and were about to return to the barrack block when this SS guard shouted, "Oh, no, you've already been counted!"

Well, there you are then—standing between that truck and that Nazi. Now, I'd nothing to lose. And it was important, of course, that you were able to talk to such a chap. If a Russian had been standing there, I wouldn't have been able to say a word. All I could have done was shake my head or something. So I said, "No, we're doctors and we're only conducting them to the truck."

But he wouldn't have it.

Fortunately for us, the block doctor came outside just at that moment and saw what was going on. He had a word with the SS man and apparently the fellow was convinced we weren't among those scheduled for gassing.

Why didn't I give that professor any drugs? Well, that, of course, is a terribly sore point for me. Because

I was scared to! Because I didn't want to put my own
life in jeopardy unnecessarily. He was going to die, anyway. And was I then to . . . yes, you do your own
reasoning, believe me. It's not at all that I'm seeking to
set a standard. But as I reasoned at the time: Was I to
risk my life for someone who had already been condemned, yes . . . condemned to death, who was *going*
to die, who was quite simply being taken to the gas
chamber? I *could* have gotten those narcotics, of course,
even though we weren't so very well stocked with
them. But we had quite a reasonable quantity of Lumi-
nal. But I *didn't do* it. *I didn't do it.*

The ward was divided into four rooms. It was almost empty, and I had been told to keep a watch along
the windows to see that no one jumped out of one. Because everything was supposed to happen cleanly, aha,
no soiled hands, no blood splashed about the place—
that wasn't in line with the system. It had to happen
cleanly.

So I was walking up and down there, and all at once
that high-ranking SS man the young boy had knelt before comes into the ward. And he sees me. And he calls
out to me. And he asks, "What are you doing there?"—
"*Was machen Sie da?*" Yes, there you have that language question again. If it had had to be in French, I
shouldn't have been able to say it so fluently. So I said
my orders were to keep an eye on the windows.

And then I could actually *see* that man thinking. I
myself, of course, was standing stiffly at attention, and

yes, I was looking at him. And I don't think I have ever been so close to death as at that moment. If I had batted an eyelid then, or had been wearing the wrong look—a smile—on my face, or had looked afraid or whatever, then one nod from him—no more, just one nod of his head—would have been enough. Apparently he didn't see anything so frightful in me, or anything unpleasant, or . . . I don't know. I don't know how I acted. Anyway, he turned on his heels and off he went. Looking back, that was the most frightening moment I experienced there.

And if he *had* nodded? I should have gone. I should have gone. But I shouldn't have gone for that one SS-er outside, to try to kill him. You were so powerless. And then that feeling comes back again, about what I said regarding Westerbork: you were in Westerbork to be put on a transport. And you were in Auschwitz to be sent to the gas chamber.

When we left the camp, on January 18, 1945, one of the motives for my not staying there or not trying to go underground was that I considered it such a victory to be leaving Auschwitz concentration camp alive. It had seemed inconceivable. When we had talked about *how* we should ever leave the camp, there had always seemed to be only one possibility: as smoke via the chimney of the gas chamber. Those selections . . . The people had become so terribly lean and so terribly ill. I once entered the ward and someone came up to me and said, "Elie, you must save me, you must save me!

They're taking me to the diarrhea station, and that's the gas chamber."

"But who are you in heaven's name?" I asked.

"I'm Jo Wolf, from Folkinge Street."

He had lived four doors away from me, we knew each other very well indeed. You just didn't recognize people anymore. I shouldn't even be able to act as a witness in a trial of SS men. If anyone were to ask me, "Show us those you recognize," I shouldn't be able to. I shouldn't recognize anyone. It is all so terribly changed. Just as in that camp the Jews changed so rapidly, owing to their physical condition, I shouldn't be able to recognize these SS men again. That man Mulka, and Kaduk, and all the rest of them there in Auschwitz.

I didn't see them at their work either. We were so terribly protected. In that camp we really lived a life apart. The life of doctors, who didn't have to go out and stand on the parade ground, who didn't go outdoors in all weathers, didn't have to stand outside in thin suits from halfpast five in the morning till eight at night (as was the case at Amersfoort). We got good food, of course. I say "of course"—but it was a fact. You looked after yourself. The soup had to be stirred, but you can stir it vertically and you can stir it horizontally. The fat was on the top and the thick lumps underneath.

I don't know whether I'm being overdramatic. I don't know, but you *do* have a very strong feeling that you, er . . . well, that you haven't er . . . that you haven't lived very nicely. But it's strange that I and a few others—perhaps quite a lot of others—should feel unhappy about it, while the men—the SS—who *forced* us to act as we did . . . haha! . . . for them it's no problem any longer. For them it's all past and done with. And that I am often still left with this problem (yes, I am often troubled by it). . . .

What I said about that professor is no sensational revelation either. I spoke about that once before, in Amsterdam, to a gathering of some Jewish science society. I tell that story, because I don't want to appear better than I am. I'm not a masochist. But these are facts. This happened. So that other people's lives . . . that I . . . yes, if you begin to reason about it. The lives of six hundred people against the life of *one* lunatic, yes, then there's no choice, you'd say. Yet it has had such an effect on me all the same that I daren't even think of euthanasia. People have sometimes asked me about it. Hitler, too, made a beginning with euthanasia . . . and that ended up with the gas chamber. It doesn't necessarily have to lead to that, but I am terribly afraid of it all the same. And I really don't dare take any stand on the matter.

Our life was a good one—"good" between inverted commas—in that place Auschwitz. There were friendships. I had one very good friend. He was called Berthold Krebs, lived in Apeldoorn, a dental mechanic. The printer of *Living Jewish Faith* (*Levend Joods Geloof*) is called Krebs too, and I often feel inclined to find out if it is the same man. But then, you're too weak

. . . I don't know why one doesn't do things like that
. . . just pick up the phone.

I became even more important. I became the "case-reporting doctor." Block 9, in which I worked for about a year, stood next to Block 10, and that was the medical experiments block for women.

It was a world of ghosts. Someone suddenly hit on the idea that the sick should take part in sports. Okay. At twelve o'clock the whole caboodle—or at least those who could walk—had to go downstairs, and then they did gymnastic exercises under the guidance of a Czech, a professor of sport. All right for him! He, with his stout and sturdy body, would give a demonstration, then they had to do it after him. . . .

We had a good time between twelve and one, if we were able to sit in the sun. And then the women from Block 10 came and took a peek round the corners. I took food to Block 10 and always had some contact. It is said—I wasn't involved myself—that there were even sexual relations there. I couldn't say. That was another remarkable thing too. Sexuality wasn't so important, even though we were getting good food. Oh yes, you masturbated, and as your physical condition declined that came to an end as well. I'd say that sex was one of the first functions to come to an end. Only hunger remains. If you're really hungry, sex doesn't count anymore.

There were certainly some plucky women in Block 10. Hilda Storosum (then Hilda van Os) told me she had refused to let them experiment on her.

"All right," they said, "in that case you'll go to Birkenau."

I saw her that day in the block when I went to take the food. And she said, "Elie, I'm facing the following problem: either to let them experiment with me or be sent to Birkenau. What ought I to do?"

I then said, "I know, but I'm not going to say. But I'll be coming back again this evening with tea. I'll hear then what you've decided."

And that evening she said, "I'm going to Birkenau."

And I said, "I thought you would too."

But it was easy, of course, for me to say that, because it was she who would be going to that terrible place, not I. Birkenau was much worse than Block 10 —if you weren't experimented on.

I want to return to that matter of the selections for the gas chamber, because that troubles my mind, of course. I've often asked myself how I should act, with the knowledge I have now, if I were in a concentration camp at the moment. I've always said, "Once is enough. I'm not going again." So that means committing suicide. For it is . . . it is not living. And then that great responsibility, guilt, at the thought that you are helping to select people for the gas chamber, for death, for transportation. As a student, as a doctor, you . . . well, you had such very different things in mind. That's a personal conflict, I believe. I don't know whether other doctors feel the same. The personal conflict—that you are struggling against your true nature, your disposition, your profession, your being, and acting differently from the way you want to act.

Hannah Arendt caused terrific resentment by saying with reference to the Eichmann trial—I was there too —that the Jewish Councils perhaps didn't merely take the work out of the Germans' hands but actually did the Germans' work for them—and did it very effectively. And not only the Jewish Councils—I think one is justified in saying this of many Jews.

In America a psychiatrist replied to her by saying that it was terribly easy for Hannah Arendt to sit behind a desk and condemn things with which she herself was never confronted. For she had fled from Germany, and then from France, and landed up in America. Well, yes, that, of course, is so. But on that basis, you could never condemn anything, unless you'd been in the same boat yourself. I have never committed rape or murder, but I can condemn them all the same. I've never been in South Africa. But yes, indeed, it does take away some of the force of your arguments and of your own convictions if you haven't experienced a thing at first hand.

Once, in Norway, I spoke to a young German, a chemist of about thirty. I didn't want to speak a single word to him at first. But we were in the same hotel for six days and once when we were sitting round the fire, a conversation got going between us. And I asked him, "What do you think about the gassing of the Jews in Nazi Germany—even if you yourself had no hand in it?"

"Yes," he said. "That wasn't right, of course, but you shouldn't forget that our towns were bombed as well. There were women and children in them too."

Well, of course, they're two different matters that

can't be compared. Yet *they* use it as a counterargu-
ment: "Sir, *you're* not in a position to judge that either."

Hannah Arendt . . . yes, she's definitely right. Let
me begin by saying quite clearly that I myself should
have done the same as those leading figures in the Jewish Council did: protect themselves first, protect their
families, protect their friends, protect their own clan.
For who were the first to be deported to Auschwitz?
That was Joe Boggs and his mate, the man behind the
apple cart, the rag-and-bone cart, who had no important
friends at all, and who spoke in a way that fetched no
response. They were the first victims. In Amsterdam,
Asscher and Cohen of the Jewish Council appear to
have said all along: We agree to this, and to that, in
order to avoid something even worse. Until in the end
they were carried off themselves.

But if Hannah Arendt were wrong, this pattern
would not have been the same all over Europe. Then
somewhere—in Poland, or in Belgium, or somewhere
else—someone would have said, "No, we're not going
to do that." What we Jewish doctors in Groningen did
wasn't so very wonderful—our refusing to examine Jews
for the concentration camps. We simply didn't do it.
But that wasn't at all important. But take a man like
Rumkovsky, the Jewish Elder in the ghetto at Lodz,
who drove through the streets in his own carriage and
spent his own money—power went to that man's head
and he had a good time of it. There are few ideal people. But from what I've read about him that Father

Titus Brandsma was one. Now there, as I see things, you had a man who never abandoned his principles to save his own skin. Well, he, of course, had a different standpoint. Like that boy in the camp at Amersfoort, he had his religion as a support. His life therefore had a basis. I wrote that in my dissertation too. I was able, of course, to see to an extent what my motives were. I could say to myself, "Look, this is your punishment. You didn't want to go to Palestine. Whatever your reasons, you preferred Holland. You thought that would be easier, and that it would afford you a better livelihood than Israel could. So now you're in this mess. If you had gone to Palestine, you wouldn't have been in it." And there you have it: we all want so terribly dearly to live; and to have a good life. And maybe we think we ourselves are more important than other people. Maybe I'm putting things too strongly, saying things which I can't always back up. But it weighs exceptionally heavy with me, personally. Hannah Arendt is the only one who has put it into words so clearly. And I must say that she may not be entirely right, but she is to a very large extent. The Germans, the *Moffen*, should have done all their dirty work themselves! Should have had to drag everybody to the trains and shove them in, without any cooperation. Who knows . . . they wouldn't have dropped the idea, of course, but it probably wouldn't all have gone off so smartly.

If there had been more sticking to principles, more people would probably have been saved. There was a large measure of cowardice, and of the urge to survive, and that made people cooperate. I thought all this out later on, I assure you. When I came out of the concentration camp I was happy, simply happy.

Presser was a man I think very highly of. He levelled terrible reproaches at the Jewish Council. I never dared write or say it to him, but he, too, benefited by the Council. He was a teacher at the Jewish High School and as a result he, too, enjoyed protection; he, too, had a special stamp against his name. Then I'm afraid of myself, you know. Knowing that I benefited from the Council too, I don't dare to criticize outright. Presser did and actually it's a pity I never asked him, "Doesn't it bother you then? You only went underground in May 1943. And you escaped with your life." (In his writings, Presser described how he was arrested and got away at the last minute with his wife. Perhaps on the grounds of the "Until further notice" stamp on his papers, as a result of which he had avoided earlier arrest. He didn't write as much, but I can well imagine it was so.)

Can't you understand then that I ask myself about him: Ought you to have voiced that criticism of the Jewish Council? It is, as a matter of fact, the only criticism I have of Presser's book. It is a first-class book and Presser was a first-class human being. A great pity such people die far too young. The documentary film about him that Bregstein made moved me to tears, it was so beautifully done.* They ought to show that on televi-

* This was a Dutch television documentary film on Professor Jacob Presser, who survived the Nazi occupation of Holland and

sion far more often. I could see it ten times over. Those
May 4 scenes, for example.

We've got as far as the journey from Auschwitz to
Mauthausen, after Auschwitz had been liberated. The
routine in Auschwitz had already become much laxer
after the gassings had ceased. We had parties. I can still
see us, lined up near Block 28 on New Year's Eve, 1944–
45. An SS guard came to count us, to see that we were
all there, and then he said, "I wish you all the best for
the coming year. In that year I shall most likely find
myself standing in your shoes and you in mine."

A word or two more about being a doctor. When
Block 9 was done away with I became, as I said, what
was known as a "case-reporting doctor." That's to say,
I was authorized to "order back" people I thought
ought to be admitted to hospital, for them to attend the
following day, and then I had to present them to the
camp doctor. All quite simple: "This man is suffering
from this or that, and I think he ought to be admitted."
And the camp doctor would then say yes or no. We
made use of this too. I had the right to admit urgent
cases in the evening, before the roll call. And it happened twice that Polish Jews came along to me and
said, "We've a very important favor to ask of you. So-
and-so may have to go on a transport and there are cer-

later became a great authority on the Jews during it. His book
Ondergang has been published (in an abbreviated version) in
English in America and elsewhere. *Ondergang* means "downfall"
or "doom," but the English title was quite different: *Ashes in
the Wind*. Published in Great Britain by The Souvenir Press,
1968. Published in the United States as *The Destruction of the
Dutch Jews* by Dutton, 1969.

tain things in Auschwitz we need him for. All you have to do is place your signature. The block doctor has been informed, everybody has been informed, that at the moment this man has a temperature of 105°. And if you'll just confirm that and sign for it, everything will be okay."

And that's what I did. I'm saying that to . . . well, not to give myself a good name, but to show that I still hadn't become completely blunted. I said to them, "I don't give a damn. You take care of it." But by then everything had become much easier, because the discipline had become much laxer and looser.

Being the case-reporting doctor meant having an important, prominent position. And how does that operate in practice? Where I live at present a doctor gets a cake sent to him after he's done a confinement. And the same sort of thing happened there as well. If I had someone admitted or said, "You must report here every morning to have your bandages done," I would at times get a bit of margarine or a chunk of sausage given to me—which I didn't, for that matter, really stand in need of.

8

End

SUDDENLY the Russians came quite a bit nearer, and on January 18, 1945, we were evacuated. The storehouses were flung open and I then selected a very good pair of shoes for myself. This turned out to be a very prudent choice, for having a solid pair of shoes proved to be one of the most important factors during that journey, through all that snow. We walked five days and slept five nights in the open air to begin with. How in God's name was it possible, at fifteen below zero? I put that in my dissertation too—that a human being can apparently stand far more than I would ever have believed possible. Though there were many who succumbed as well, of course. I can still recall how we arrived at some spot and had to line up.

"We'll be getting soup now," we said.

And it turned out that there was a water tap there somewhere, with a very long hose-pipe attached to it. And we were allowed to drink as much water as we wanted. After that we traveled for five days in open coal wagons. And then one night I appear to have gone completely off my head. Someone I know well told me about it afterward. I don't remember a thing myself. But I wanted to jump out of that coal wagon, and they held me back.

As daylight returned I came round again. It was an obsession, of course—standing there all the time with a good hundred men in a coal wagon. The tough guys sat down and were able to keep the others at a distance. It was a very nasty journey, that was. We crossed the Czech frontier near Godesberg, if I'm right, and men and women were standing there and they threw loaves and apples and so on into the wagons. That made a very deep impression on me.

We arrived in Mauthausen. I went back to that camp once. It is still exactly the same, a very good monument of its kind. But by then I had lost my fear of the place. Unjustifiably—but that's how it was. From Mauthausen to Melk. I went downhill then. I was no longer set to work as a doctor but had to go out with the ordinary labor squads. At night, out of doors, shoveling gravel into trucks which were then driven inside a mountain, for they were building underground factories there. I succeeded in getting inside there too— at least you were then out of the frost—and then I became an assistant to a carpenter. That was fine, that was. I walked round after him with a box of tools. But then he said to me, "*Gib mir zwei Keile.*" *Keile* are wedges, but I didn't know that and gave him a chopper.

Then the chap said, "I said wedges, didn't I? And *he* wants to be a carpenter!"

I didn't at all. But I was sacked on the spot, anyway. I was no good for the job.

I worked hard there, very hard, shoveling gravel, shoveling cement. And the "days" were long. You had to go on parade at six in the evening and didn't come back till seven o'clock the next morning. And it seemed that night would never end. An hour in a concentration camp is like an eternity in ordinary life, I think. And it was so terribly cold there. I truly did think then that I should not be able to keep going so very much longer.

I got to that stage in Ebensee. We went from Melk to Ebensee in river barges. And then the end really did come in sight. I began to work out for myself how many calories I needed and how many I was getting. And I made a wager with myself that I could hold out till mid-May. Well, we were liberated on May 6, by General Patton's Third Army.

How do you act at such a moment? I walked on the parade ground with my arms held high—so I was still able to walk—and I shouted, "Freedom! Freedom!" And then we stormed the SS storehouses. And what did I take? I didn't take food. I took a typewriter, paper, and envelopes. For I wanted to write. Very strange. A few of the other prisoners saw me hauling that heavy thing around and wanted to know what was inside. A typewriter. They were very disappointed. They had thought that I had a whole load of food with me. No, I didn't write anything. I was really at lowest ebb.

And now? It's as good as impossible to live unaffected anymore. Yes, but it's the same for everyone who has gone through these things. They have left their mark on us and there's no wiping that mark off. But well, it is, God dammit, terribly bad, I mean . . . oh, God, God . . . I once spoke to an audience of doctors about it. I said to them, "Sometimes I've sat in the canteen with you, and once there was one who said, 'My son took his doctor's intermediate yesterday.' And then I went back in my mind and thought, I might have been able to say that as well. And then I walked away. I went and sat in my car and wept." And I said to them, "I don't doubt you'll have said to yourselves, 'What a queer type that Cohen chap is. Whatever did we say wrong?' Nothing. Nothing anti-Semitic. Do you follow any of this? I just *couldn't* bear it."

I can't reconcile myself to being faced with the problems of the children of my second marriage—it's to be hoped their health will be spared—but their place in society, their studies, a friend or a boy friend, a marriage or whatever. I still feel sore about it—that I should still be confronted with problems like this, that normally play a part at forty-five or fifty. If you have a normal marriage, that is. It ought not to be necessary now. And it's a particularly heavy burden to me. After all, I don't stand much chance of seeing it through for many more decades. My daughter, Naomi, is now twenty and training to be a social worker. When she has finished, she will have a profession by which she can earn a living. That will put my mind at rest. And naturally I hope she will one day become a happy wife and mother. My boy is now sixteen. Yesterday we had a few people visiting us. Among them were medical students with fathers who are also doctors. Then I took a look at Dan, my boy, and thought: If things go well, he's now got another year and a half to do at high school, then study medicine for seven or eight years. Then two years military service. That makes ten to eleven years. By then I'll be well over seventy. So, shall I ever see it all?

And that, of course, is resentment at your fate, at my fate in life. My wife says I am ungrateful. She's right there. Everyone is completely right who shows me . . . well, who shows me how wrong I am. But being wrong in this particular way is a very difficult business. You can try to reason it all away, but the emotional side of it always keeps breaking through again. It does play a part, it *does* have an effect. It isn't at all true that, as an older type of parent, you're so much wiser than you would have been if you had been showing your children the way twenty years ago. And this is what I still resent so very much. That I should still constantly be wrestling with this problem. Yes, wrestling with it, because, after all, you want to see them grow up into worthy people. And I should so very much like to see them go to Israel. Do the thing I failed to do myself. Yes, I think that's terrible, terrible. . . .

Shall we stop?